| DATE |  |  |  |
|---|---|---|---|
|  |  |  |  |
|  |  |  |  |
|  |  |  |  |
|  |  |  |  |
|  |  |  |  |
|  |  |  |  |
|  |  |  |  |
|  |  |  |  |
|  |  |  |  |
|  |  |  |  |
|  |  |  |  |
|  |  |  |  |
|  |  |  |  |
|  |  |  |  |

# Women
# Pioneers
# of Science

*by the same author*

Black Pioneers of Science
and Invention

# Women Pioneers of Science

*by Louis Haber*

Harcourt Brace Jovanovich, Publishers
San Diego  New York  London

Printed in the United States of America

Library of Congress Cataloging in Publication Data

Haber, Louis.
Women pioneers of science.

Bibliography: p.
Includes index.
SUMMARY: Biographies of 12 women pioneers and
leaders in a variety of scientific fields.
1. Women scientists—Biography—Juvenile literature.
2. Women in science—Juvenile literature.
[1. Women scientists. 2. Scientists] I. Title.
Q141.H215      509'.2'2 [B]      [920]      79–87517
ISBN 0–15–299202–2

B C D E

*To*
Blanche
Rikki
Jacky

# Contents

Author's Note  xi

Foreword  xiii

I  Women in Science  3

II  Dr. Alice Hamilton  12
(1869–1970)  Industrial Medicine

III  Dr. Florence Rena Sabin  30
(1871–1953)  Public Health Physician

IV  Dr. Lise Meitner  41
(1878–1968)  Nuclear Physicist

V  Dr. Leta S. Hollingworth  52
(1886–1939)  Educational Psychologist

VI  Dr. Rachel Fuller Brown  63
(1898–  )  Biochemist

VII  Dr. Gladys Anderson Emerson  73
(1903–  )  Biochemist and Nutritionist

Contents

VIII   Dr. Maria Goeppert Mayer   83
(1906–1972)   Nuclear Physicist

IX   Dr. Myra Adele Logan   97
(1909–1977)   Physician and Surgeon

X   Dr. Dorothy Crowfoot Hodgkin   105
(1910–    )   Crystallographer

XI   Dr. Jane C. Wright   117
(1920–    )   Physician and Chemotherapist

XII   Dr. Rosalyn S. Yalow   128
(1921–    )   Nuclear Physicist in Medicine

XIII   Dr. Sylvia Earle Mead   141
(1935–    )   Marine Biologist

Professional Women's Groups   155

Bibliography   159

Index   167

Contents

x

# Author's Note

This book describes the lives and important contributions of some of the outstanding women in the fields of science. It is by no means meant to be a complete treatment and, in fact, makes up less than one percent of such women. The task of selecting the women scientists to be included in this book was indeed a most difficult one! They were chosen as typical models of the kind of women scientists worth imitating. An attempt was also made to represent as many fields of science as possible, and preference was given to current scientists for the most part.

The false doctrine of the superiority of men over women, sponsored by society for centuries, now looms as a major part of the reason for the inadequacy of men in meeting women as equal human beings to solve the problems of co-existence.

Contacts with scientists now living and with relatives of scientists provided valuable first-hand materials, and the author is most grateful to Dr. Jane C. Wright, Dr. Rosalyn S. Yalow, Dr. Rachel F. Brown, Dr. Gladys A. Emerson, Dr. Dorothy C. Hodgkin, Dr. Sylvia E. Mead, Dr. Joseph Mayer (husband of Maria G. Mayer), Mrs. Aida Winters (sister-in-law of Dr. Myra Logan), and Harold Logan (Dr. Logan's brother).

Special thanks are due Barbara Lucas, my editor, for her thoughtful and extremely helpful suggestions and encouragement, and her skill in turning the manuscript into this book. Thanks also to my son, Richard, and my daughter-in-law, Jacky, for their reading and helpful criticism of several of the chapters in this book. The author is most grateful to his wife, Blanche, for her encouragement and reading and constructively criticising early drafts of the chapters.

*Author's Note*

# Foreword

*. . . it would be socially logical to deny women . . .*
*places . . . in our medical schools . . .*
—DR. ALFRED P. INGEGNO

One might accept the above statement as having been made a hundred years ago or even fifty. The fact is it was made in an article published in a medical journal in 1961. It was not until two years later that most medical schools in the United States were to open their doors to women students.

Six women have won the coveted Nobel Prize in the fields of science in this century, yet few scientists, let alone laymen, are able to name more than one of them—Marie Curie, who was the first woman scientist to win the award. She and her husband, Pierre, shared the prize in physics in 1903 for the discovery and isolation of a new element, radium. That same year Pierre Curie refused the French Legion of Honor because it was offered only to him and not to Marie. Marie Curie also discovered another new chemical element, which she named polonium (after her native Poland). In 1911 she received a second Nobel Prize in chemistry. She was acclaimed and honored by scientists and statesmen all over the world.

The second woman to receive the Nobel Prize in the sciences was Irène Joliot-Curie (1897–1956), the daughter of Marie Curie, who shared the prize in chemistry with her husband, Frédéric Joliot, in 1935. They had continued the research on radioactivity begun by Marie Curie and got the prize for their discovery of artificially created radioisotopes (radioactive forms of atoms produced by bombarding nonradioactive elements with alpha particles in a cyclotron) and transmutation of atoms (changing one chemical element into another by bombardment with atomic particles).

Gerty Theresa Cori (1896–1957) was the third woman and the first American woman to receive the Nobel Prize. She shared it with her husband, Carl, in the field of medicine and physiology in 1947. Their work involved the metabolism of carbohydrates in the human body, particularly with the way in which glycogen is converted to glucose. Their research also included the mechanism of the action of hormones in the body.

Maria Goeppert Mayer (1906–1972) was the fourth woman to win the Nobel Prize and the first to receive it in theoretical physics in 1963. (See Chapter 8.) The following year, 1964, saw the Nobel Prize awarded to the British chemist Dorothy Crowfoot Hodgkin (born 1910). (See Chapter X.) The sixth and latest woman to win the Nobel Prize was Rosalyn S. Yalow (born 1921) of the Bronx Veterans Administration Hospital. Although not a physician, she won the prize in 1977 in medicine and physiology. (See Chapter XII.)

Rosalind Franklin, a young and talented crystallographer, missed being awarded the Nobel Prize by her unfortunate early death at the age of thirty-seven. The prize is awarded only to living persons. She and Maurice Wilkins were trying to determine the structure of the DNA (deoxyribose nucleic acid) by means of X-ray diffraction. An explanation of this method may be found on page 110. Knowledge of the structure of the DNA molecule is enormously helpful in the study of heredity. When the Nobel Prize was awarded in 1962 to J. D. Watson, F. H. Crick, and M. Wilkins for the discovery of the structure of the DNA molecule, Rosalind Franklin did not share in the credit nor in the Nobel Prize, although her basic work made the discovery possible.

The important role played by women in the development of scientific progress in the United States and in the world has still not become an integral part of science education in our schools. Science textbooks and other science books commonly used in the schools contain little information dealing with the contributions of women to the fields of science. While frequent references are made to Marie Curie and her work, the lack of reference to other women scientists would make it appear that they do not exist. Important and significant contributions made by women are not known to the average science teacher and consequently to the science student.

It was not so long ago that it was felt that women had smaller brains than men, and less intelligence, that women were more emotional and unstable; in a crisis you could always rely on them to swoon or become otherwise helpless; they were weak and sickly creatures; they had little judgment and less sense; they could not be entrusted with the handling of money.

The greatest exposure of these myths was made during World War I, when, for the first time, women were called upon to replace men in occupations which were formerly the exclusive preserve of men. They became bus drivers, conductors, factory workers, farm workers, laborers, supervisors, executive officers, and a great many other things at which many had believed they could not work. By the time the war was over many employers were reluctant to exchange their women employees for men. For women, the period from 1918 to 1939 was essentially one of consolidation of gains so that by the time World War II broke out there was no hesitation on the part of anyone in calling upon women to serve in the civilian roles of men and, in many cases, also in the armed services.

Early in the 1900s Sir Cyril Burt, the British founder of educational psychology, concluded that racial differences in intelligence test scores were the result of heredity. He also concluded that Jews and Irish were less intelligent than the English and that *men were smarter than women.* New findings, reported by Professor D. D. Dorfman of the University of Iowa, clearly show that the results of IQ tests supposedly given by Burt were "faked" by him. In Professor Dorfman's words, Burt's statistics "had been fabricated."

Dr. Leta Hollingworth of Columbia University, whose work is outlined in this book, did much to disprove scientifically any ideas of men being in any way superior to women.

It is curious that we should so readily accept the reality of a woman as chief executive of a country, such as Queen Elizabeth of Great Britain, Queen Juliana of the Netherlands, and Prime Minister Golda Meir of Israel, yet be outraged at the very thought of a woman President of the United States. It is interesting, however, that in response to the question by the Gallup Poll "Would you support a woman for President?" in 1937, 31 percent said yes; in 1970, 53 percent said yes; and in 1975, 73 percent said yes. The Gallup Poll also reported that seven out of ten Americans think the country would be better governed if more women held public office.

In her speech in Stockholm, Sweden, accepting the Nobel Prize, Dr. Rosalyn Yalow stated, "The world cannot afford the loss of the talents of half of its people if we are to solve the many problems which beset us."

The truth will make men free as well as women. Until women are freed from the myths which at present impede their progress, no man can be free or mentally completely healthy. The liberation of woman means the liberation of man.

# Women
# Pioneers
# of Science

# I

## Women in Science

Women's contributions to the sciences did not begin with Madame Curie's work in the nineteenth century. It began long before that. In the Roman Empire, during the second century, Aspasia was a doctor who specialized in obstetrics, gynecology, and surgery. She performed a variety of surgical operations and wrote a great deal about the practice of medicine. The earliest medical school in Salerno, Italy, in the eleventh century had women professors on its faculty. One of these women, Trotula, wrote books on gynecology which were studied for 500 years. She has been regarded as one of the greatest medical women of Italian history. She was skilled at surgery and could lance an abscess, perform a Caesarian section, and repair a rupture. Her book discussed the hygiene of pregnancy and childbirth, the treatment of sterility, the care of newborn babies, the treatment of skin ailments, and ways to improve the complexion.

Manuscripts and early printed works in France and England contain many pictures of hospital scenes in which women doctors are shown actively at work. In the reign of England's Henry VIII, when physicians, surgeons, and midwives were required to be licensed, women as well as men obtained these licenses. The daughter of Sir Thomas More was a physician at this time.

An interesting story unfolded in England in the nineteenth century. James Barry (1797–1865) was awarded the medical degree from the University of Edinburgh in 1812 at the age of fifteen. Dr. Barry joined the British army in 1813 as hospital assistant and was promoted to assistant surgeon as a reward for distinguished service during the Battle of Waterloo. Dr. Barry served as inspector general of the British army from 1856 to 1865, the highest medical position in the army, and saw service in Europe, South Africa, Canada, Jamaica, and India. Dr. Barry died in July 1865, and when an autopsy was performed, "he" was found to have been a woman! She had spent more than fifty years as a member of an elite army officer corps without her secret's being penetrated. Even her male servant, who had accompanied her to many parts of the British Empire, did not know. The War Office and the British Medical Association were dismayed at what the autopsy revealed. However, the problem was solved. It was simply decreed that she was a man, so stated in the death certificate, and so inscribed on her tombstone. By popular account, she was the illegitimate daughter of the Prince Regent (the future King George IV of England) and a well-known Scottish lady.

On numerous occasions women authors would conceal their sex, as, for example, Amandine Aurore Lucie Dupin, who sent her manuscripts to the publisher under the name of "George Sand," and Marian Evans, who sent hers under the pseudonym of "George Eliot." Few men ever chose to send their manuscripts to a publisher under feminine pseudonyms.

Women were also responsible for various types of

inventions that were patented by the government. The first woman to receive a patent in the United States was Mary Kies, who won a patent on May 5, 1809, for a process of straw weaving with silk or thread. A government report in 1888 credited women with more than one thousand patents, including the pneumatic tire, heating and ventilating apparatus for buildings, railroad cars, air-cooling fans, digging machines, a snow plow, stage scenery, paving blocks, and fire escapes. By far the most remarkable of women's inventions during the period 1841–1851 was a submarine telescope and lamp, for which a patent was awarded in 1845 to Sarah Mather.

In the eighteenth century an American woman by the name of Catherine Greene is said to have developed a plan for a machine to separate cotton from its seeds—the cotton gin. Under her direction an employee, Eli Whitney, constructed the machine. Fearful of public scorn, she did not apply for the patent, and Whitney has been credited with the invention.

In the United States both men and women engaged in medical practice in the early days of our history. Training was largely by apprenticeship. Babies were mostly delivered by midwives, who were required to take an oath "to be kind to the poor as well as to the rich, and not listen to lies as to the father of a baby, nor conceal the birth of bastards, nor produce miscarriages, nor operate needlessly on any woman." The mother of William Lloyd Garrison supported her children by midwifery while trying at the same time to abolish slavery and emancipate women.

As medicine became more scientific, women and barbers were specifically excluded. The first medical college in the United States was set up in Philadelphia in 1765.

*Women in Science*

Elizabeth Blackwell was the first "petticoat physician" in the United States. Born in Bristol, England, in 1821, the third of nine children, she had a father who believed in the equality of the sexes. When Elizabeth was eleven, the family came to America. Her father died while she was in her teens, and Elizabeth opened a "school for young ladies" to earn a livelihood. At age twenty-four she was permitted to be the assistant of a Philadelphia physician, and she began to fix her sights on a medical career. One doctor told her, "You might as well lead a revolution as try to be a physician." She applied at a number of medical schools and was refused by every one. Finally, she was accepted at the Geneva Medical College (now Hobart College) through an unusual action by the student body. For a time she was barred from classes which discussed subjects "too indelicate for a lady." Medical school then was a two-year course, and in 1849 Elizabeth became the first woman to be granted a degree by an American medical school.

Since no hospital would permit Elizabeth to continue her training, she went to Paris, where she was accepted at La Maternité, a center for training midwives. After that she returned to the United States to set up private practice. In 1857 Elizabeth and her sister, Emily, now also a doctor, founded the New York Infirmary for Women and Children (now the New York Infirmary). This was the first hospital in the United States where women medical students could get practical instruction. It was also the first hospital to have an all-women staff in both the medical and the surgical departments; the first to supply a home visitor (visiting nurse today) to attend poor patients in their homes; and the first to require a four-year course of study. It was not until after World War II that

*Women Pioneers of Science*

women were permitted to intern in most other hospitals in this country.

The first distinguished medical school to become coeducational was Johns Hopkins University in 1893. This was because Mary Elizabeth Garrett, who had raised one half million dollars to enable the school to be completed, gave the money on the condition that the school admit women on the same terms as men. Florence Rena Sabin (see Chapter III) was admitted and subsequently became the first woman ever to become a full professor at Johns Hopkins.

Emily Dunning Barringer broke through the final barrier of hospital training of women. She was the first woman to swing herself onto the high steps of a horse-drawn city ambulance in New York City, a feat she performed with grace and propriety in a specially tailored divided riding skirt.

Dr. Mary Edwards Walker was the first female surgeon in the United States Army and served during the Civil War. President Andrew Johnson presented the Medal of Honor to Dr. Walker on November 11, 1865, in recognition of her zeal and valor in tending the troops. General William T. Sherman had recommended the medal, and President Lincoln had signed the testimonial before his death. Dr. Walker was a lifelong suffragette, and from the time of the Civil War, she wore men's trousers and frock coats. She would give feminist lectures attired in full men's evening dress, with the Medal of Honor dangling on her left lapel. She had spent four months in a Confederate prison during the war and was exchanged "man for man" for a Confederate major.

Throughout the ages, women in medicine have had to face prejudice and male chauvinism. When Elizabeth

Blackwell was graduated from the Geneva Medical School, the *Boston Medical & Surgical Journal* commented, "It is to be regretted that she has been induced to depart from the appropriate sphere of her sex and led to aspire to honors and duties which, by the order of nature and the common consent of the world, devolve alone upon men." More recently, on December 4, 1961, in an article in *Medical Economics* titled "The Case Against Female M.D.'s," Dr. Alfred P. Ingegno states, "I get sick and tired of ridiculous statements about helping solve the alleged physician shortage by having more women physicians. This might be a good solution if the only alternative to it were no physicians at all. But why not solve the problem more efficiently by having more men physicians? In fact, it would be socially logical to deny women even the five or six percent of places now given to them in our medical schools. Let's not allow our love and respect for the ladies to blind us to the relative waste of giving them medical training."

Most hospitals in the country now will appoint women as interns and residents, and although it is still difficult for a woman to be named to a top hospital post, this too does happen. At the Arkansas University Medical School and Hospital, for instance, the chief resident in 1964 was not only a woman but a black woman. This is the same medical school which made history in 1948, when it became the first in the South since Reconstruction days to admit a black woman student. In 1967 Dr. Jane Wright, another black woman, was appointed associate dean of the New York Medical College in New York City. The first black woman doctor in the country was Rebecca Lee, who was graduated from the New England Female Medical

College in 1864 and set up practice in Richmond, Virginia, that same year.

The contributions that women have made in the fields of science are many and varied. Maria Mitchell, in 1847, discovered a new comet by means of her telescope. For this she received a medal from King Frederick VII of Denmark and became the first woman to be admitted to the American Academy of Arts and Sciences. She taught astronomy at Vassar College for twenty-three years.

Ellen Swallow (1842–1911) created the profession of home economics. She was a chemist who was a leader in applied and domestic science. An instructor in sanitary chemistry at the Massachusetts Institute of Technology, she taught her students how to analyze water, sewage, and air for harmful chemicals. She worked out courses of study for public schools, colleges, and agricultural schools in home economics and organized the American Home Economics Association. She also established the *Journal of Home Economics*.

Rachel Carson (1907–1964) was an ecologist who shook the scientific world with the publication of her now-famous book *Silent Spring*. In this book Carson warned of the tremendous dangers to the environment and to people that accompany the use of such insecticides as DDT and others like it. She objected not only to the indiscriminate use of pesticides but also to an irresponsible industrial society. Her book opened the door to legislative action restricting the use of pesticides.

Lucy Hobbs Taylor (1833–1910) of the United States was the world's first woman to attend and graduate from a dental school, the Ohio Dental School, in 1866.

Margaret Maltby (1860–1944) was a physicist who was

the first American woman to receive a doctorate degree from Göttingen University in Germany. She did research on chemical solutions and radioactivity and taught at Barnard College in New York City from 1900 to 1931.

Helen Brooke Taussig (born 1898) is a physician who specializes in congenital malformations of the heart and was the codeveloper of the "blue baby" operation in 1944. She was the first physician to alert this country to the dangers of thalidomide in the production of malformed babies (1962). She was also the first to demonstrate that changes in the heart and lungs could be diagnosed by X-rays and the fluoroscope.

Dr. Susan McKinney Steward was one of the first black women doctors in the United States, receiving her medical degree in 1870 from the New York Medical College & Hospital for Women. To appreciate this achievement fully, it must be realized that the Civil War had ended only six years before, that there were very few black male doctors at the time, and very few female doctors of any race. Two years ago black women doctors in this country formed a society, the aims of which are to aid young black women medical students and to document the achievements of black physicians. The name of the new society is the Susan Smith McKinney Steward Medical Society. Dr. May E. Chinn, one of the society's founders, recalls that her father, who had been a slave, opposed her even going to college. But her mother, who "scrubbed floors and hired out as a cook," became the driving force behind her educational effort. She was the first black woman graduate of the University of Bellevue Medical Center and the first to intern in 1926 at the then predominantly white Harlem Hospital. The hospital is now mostly black.

*Women Pioneers of Science*

Dr. Margaret Mead (1901–1978) was one of America's foremost anthropologists. Lecturer, columnist, and writer, she was also a keen critic of modern America, concerned with juvenile delinquency, abortion laws, drug addiction, world peace, family planning, careers for women, and the population explosion. She was one of the first to go directly to existing primitive cultures and bring back eyewitness reports. In this way she brought about major modifications in the once-accepted conclusions regarding primitive life.

Now let us look more closely at the lives of some of these remarkable women and the significant contributions they made to the fields of science.

# II

## Dr. Alice Hamilton

### Industrial Medicine

Pioneer in industrial medicine and the first woman to teach at the medical school of Harvard University (1919–1935)—this tells only part of the story of the extraordinary Dr. Alice Hamilton. When she was a child, her mother said to her, "There are two kinds of people in the world, the ones who say, 'Somebody ought to do something about that but why should I?' and those who say, 'Somebody must do something about that, then why not I?'" Alice chose the latter course and went on to perform what some of her colleagues called miracles in her hundred and one years of life.

Born in New York City on February 27, 1869, she spent her childhood in Fort Wayne, Indiana. She and her three sisters were all born within six years' time, while her one brother was born when Alice was seventeen years old. She was greatly influenced by her grandmother, who campaigned for women's suffrage and was a personal friend of Susan B. Anthony's. As a teenager Alice planned to become a medical missionary after reading a description of Persia in a book. She chose medicine because "as a doctor I could go anywhere I pleased, to far off lands or city slums, and be quite sure that I could be of use anywhere."

Since her father did not approve of public schools, all the children were taught at home. At the age of seventeen Alice left home for the first time to go away to school. She went to Miss Porter's School in Framington, Connecticut, for two years, which was traditional for the Hamilton girls. "The teaching we received was the world's worst." Afterward she studied physics and chemistry with a private teacher, studied medicine for one year in Fort Wayne, and then entered the medical school of the University of Michigan at Ann Arbor. It was very difficult for women at that time to be admitted to medical schools, and once there women met all kinds of discrimination. According to the school's catalogue, "Practical anatomy is pursued by the two sexes in separate rooms and some of the lectures and demonstrations which it is not desirable to present to the two sexes together are given to them separately."

Alice received her medical degree in 1893 at the age of twenty-four. Although few internships were open to women, Dr. Hamilton managed to spend two months in the Hospital for Women and Children in Minneapolis and nine months in the New England Hospital for Women and Children outside Boston. She became interested in pathology, a medical specialty dealing with diseased organs and cells of the body and usually involving examinations of dead people to determine the cause of death (an autopsy). Her professor at Ann Arbor told her, she said, "If I hoped to devote myself to pathology I must study in Germany, otherwise I should never be accepted as an expert." So in 1895 Dr. Hamilton went to Germany.

In Germany she experienced great difficulty in being

*Dr. Alice Hamilton*

allowed to attend lectures and courses because she was a woman. Her teachers and fellow students there held her in contempt "because I was a woman and an American, therefore uneducated and incapable of real study." She remained in Germany for one year and then returned to the United States.

Then came the day that was to change Dr. Hamilton's life. Jane Addams came to speak in the Methodist Church in Fort Wayne. Dr. Hamilton went to hear her and was tremendously impressed. Miss Addams spoke about Hull House in Chicago, a settlement house founded in 1889. Dr. Hamilton was determined to be near Jane Addams, and in 1897 she became a resident of Hull House, where she was to remain for the next twenty-two years.

Hull House had a day nursery, a kindergarten, public baths, and a playground and was located in the slums of Chicago. Alice Hamilton opened a baby clinic, which soon was taking in the older brothers and sisters up to eight years of age. She worked with the poor and the immigrants who lived there and became involved in labor's causes and the unions, often helping on picket lines when there was a strike.

Her first paying job was teaching pathology at the Women's Medical College of Northwestern University in Chicago. She was thrilled at the chance of being in Chicago near Hull House and Jane Addams. She changed the teaching of pathology at the Women's Medical College from only lectures and reading to actual laboratory work with specimens and slides from autopsies.

In 1902 an epidemic of typhoid fever struck Chicago, and Hull House was the center of the hardest-struck region. Flies were carrying the typhoid germs, and the water, drawn for drinking from the nearby lake, was not chlorinated. Dr. Hamilton went around collecting flies from kitchens and toilets. She dropped them into tubes of broth and incubated the tubes. She found typhoid germs and wrote up her findings for publication. The effect was gratifying. Public pressure resulted in a complete reorganization of the Health Department under a new chief. A break was discovered in the pipes carrying drinking water, and sewage was escaping into the water. Action was quickly taken to correct these conditions, thanks to the alert efforts made by Alice Hamilton.

Some ten years after coming to Hull House, she became active in the birth control movement. She saw what hardships unlimited childbearing meant to a poor community. She also saw the horrible results of self-inflicted abortions.

Living in Hull House, in a working-class quarter, and coming into contact with workers and their wives, Dr. Hamilton could not help hearing tales of the dangers workingmen faced, of cases of carbon monoxide gassing in the great steel mills, of painters disabled by lead poisoning, of pneumonia and rheumatism among the men in the stockyards. Illinois, and for that matter most of the other states, had no legislation providing compensation for accidents or diseases caused by occupation. While industrial medicine was a recognized branch of the medical sciences in most European countries, it did not exist in the United States. The American Medical Association never devoted a meeting to this subject, and no medical men specialized in industrial medicine.

Dr. Hamilton saw many of the results of occupational disease in men whose homes she visited while at Hull House. She became interested in the "dangerous trades." Nobody was concerned about occupational diseases, so

*Dr. Alice Hamilton*

she decided to make it her concern. Up to that time there was no legal protection for workers in the United States, as there was in European countries.

A number of workers in Chicago were employed in match factories. The matches were made with phosphorus, and the air in these factories was filled with phosphorus fumes that were breathed in by the men and women who worked there. These workers developed "phossy jaw," a disease caused by the phosphorus penetrating the teeth, killing the roots, and injuring the jawbone. Abscesses would then form, the pain was intense, and the jawbone would have to be surgically removed. As a result, the face would be horribly disfigured. At best the worker would have to live on liquid food for the rest of his life. These facts were made public by Alice Hamilton and others in 1909, and protests were made. This led to the substitution of sesquisulfide, a harmless substance, for the poisonous phosphorus. After that substitution was made, "phossy jaw" disappeared from American match factories.

Dr. Hamilton's opportunity came in 1910, when Governor Charles Deneen of Illinois appointed her director of an Occupational Disease Commission to survey industrial diseases in the state, write a report, and formulate recommendations for the Illinois legislature. This was the first time a state had ever undertaken such a survey. She had the assistance of twenty young doctors, medical students, and social workers. She chose lead poisoning for her own special study. She personally visited many of the lead industries, studied hospital records of men with lead poisoning, and interviewed labor leaders, doctors, and druggists in working-class quarters. She talked to the wives of men who worked in lead factories. She discov-

*Dr. Alice Hamilton*

ered that the men were being poisoned by breathing in lead dust and lead fumes. The answer was simple. Air in the factory must be kept free of lead dust and fumes. Resistance, however, on the part of the factory owners was great, as it is today. It cost money!

Dr. Hamilton wrote articles and made speeches pleading for the recognition of lead poisoning as a real and serious medical problem. She described the terrible symptoms of lead poisoning—the hanging head, bowed shoulders, hands that hung limply and could hardly be raised, trembling movements of the muscles of the body, paralysis, and extreme loss of weight. A young Italian worked for one month in a white lead plant. There was a great deal of dust in his work. One day he was seized with an agonizing pain in his head which came upon him so suddenly that he fell to the ground. He was sent to the hospital semiconscious with convulsive attacks and was there for two weeks. When he came home, he had a relapse and had to go back to the hospital. Three months later he was still in poor health and could not do a full day's work.

The International Congress on Occupational Accidents and Diseases held a conference in Brussels, Belgium, and Alice Hamilton was sent to attend. She took the opportunity to visit lead plants in England and on the Continent. At the meeting she reported on the white lead industry in the United States. She was unable, however, during the question period, to answer questions such as "What legal regulations does the United States have for the dangerous trades?" A representative from the Belgian Labor Department said, "It is well known that there is no industrial hygiene in the United States. It does not exist." Charles O'Neill, commissioner of labor in the United

States, also attended this meeting, and when Dr. Hamilton returned home, he asked her to undertake, for the federal government, a survey first of the lead trades and then of other poisonous trades. The offer was accepted at once.

The first industry she investigated was the production of white lead, which was regarded as the most dangerous of the lead trades. It involved the handling of dry white lead, and the men worked in an atmosphere filled with poisonous lead dust. Convulsions, called lead fits, and insanity were common among these workers. (The expression "mad hatters" from the book *Alice in Wonderland* refers to the fact that lead substances were used in the processing of felt for hats, and as a result, many hatters became insane.) Dr. Hamilton inspected factories in Omaha, St. Louis, Cincinnati, Pittsburgh, New York, and Philadelphia. The story was the same in all of them—crowded, dark, ill-ventilated, dilapidated, dusty processes. There was little or no concern for the health of the men. It was taken for granted that the majority would quit after a few months.

In one white lead plant that Dr. Hamilton visited, she found the place dreadful—old, covered with the dust of years, and no attempt made to control any of the obvious dangers. She was then taken to the plant owner's stable nearby, where beautiful horses were standing on a clean brick floor, eating from clean mangers, and rubbed down till their coats shone. "Mr. B. is awful proud of his horses. He thinks nothing is too good for them."

Another industry using lead was the making and enameling of bathtubs. Here is Dr. Hamilton's description of what she saw in one of these plants: "In front of the great furnace stood the enameler and his helper. The door

*Dr. Alice Hamilton*

19

swung open and, with the aid of a mechanism, a red-hot bathtub was lifted out. The enameler then dredged as quickly as possible powdered enamel (containing lead) over the hot surface where it melted and flowed to form an even coating. His helper stood beside him working the turntable on which the tub stood so as to present all its inner surface to the enameler. The men during this procedure were in a thick cloud of lead dust and were breathing rapidly and deeply because of the exertion and the extreme heat. When the coat was applied, the tub was swung back into the furnace and then there would be a few minutes for the men to relax, to go to the window for a breath of fresh air, or to take a bite of lunch. There was never any break in the shift so the men had the choice between fasting and eating their lunch with lead-covered hands in a lead-laden atmosphere."

Today diagnosis of lead poisoning includes chemical and microscopic blood tests, chemical tests of body excretions, delicate tests for nerve responses, as well as physical examination. Dr. Hamilton had to depend on seeing the lead line, a deposit of black lead sulfide in the cells of the lining of the mouth, usually clearest on the gum along the margin of the front teeth. She examined 148 enamelers and found 54 were "leaded" while 38 were "probable cases." The foreman of the enameling factory told her, "They don't last long at it. Four years at the most, then they quit and go home to the old country."

"To die?" she asked.

"Well, I suppose that is about the size of it," he replied.

Seventeen years later, in 1929, Dr. Hamilton returned to the bathtub plant to make a second survey. The risk of lead poisoning had been somewhat moderated, but by then silicosis had become the most important of the industrial diseases. Tubs from the foundry have a smooth surface, and enamel does not stick to it. To make the enamel stick, the surface of the tubs is roughened with a blast of fine sand. As a result, the room in which the men sandblasted the tubs would be filled with great clouds of fine sand which the men breathed in. The fine sand got into the delicate lungs, doing horrible damage and causing the formation of fibrous tissue called silicosis.

In one smelter refinery where lead poisoning was widespread, no attempt was made to protect the workers from the harmful dust and fumes. In the event of an accident, the company doctor would prevent a lawsuit by certifying that the victim had had heart disease and it was an attack of heart failure on the part of the worker and therefore no negligence on the part of the company. Ironically the doctor's salary was paid by the men, from whose wages $1.75 was deducted every month for "medical care."

One of Dr. Hamilton's success stories has to do with the painting trade. In this trade there were two poisons that threatened the health of a painter—lead and turpentine. In European countries the use of white lead paint on the *inside* of buildings was forbidden. Dr. Hamilton observed acute cases of lead poisoning among painters who worked on the inside of Pullman cars. She told this to Jane Addams, who told it to Mrs. Joseph T. Bowen, a wealthy woman who was a large holder of Pullman stock. Mrs. Bowen made a formal protest, and Alice Hamilton was called to present the case to Pullman officials. She later said, "Changes took place with breathtaking speed." By the end of 1912 there was a modern surgical department, an eye specialist, and a medical department to supervise the five hundred painters. A less dangerous

*Dr. Alice Hamilton*

form of lead was used in the paint, and every effort was made to protect the men against the lead dust. Results were striking! In 1912 there had been 109 cases of lead poisoning among 489 men during the first six months, but in 1913 only 3 cases were found in a year among 639 men. Since then lead paint has been almost entirely eliminated. Lead is now replaced by iron oxides and titanium oxide, which are quite harmless.

Some of the states began passing laws providing compensation for workers coming down with certain industrial diseases, no doubt stimulated by the kind of public awareness brought about by Dr. Hamilton's activities. Companies took out insurance to protect themselves. The insurance companies, to protect their own interests, insisted on preventative measures in the factories they insured. In this way, too, progress is made.

In 1914 World War I broke out in Europe, and Dr. Hamilton was put to work by the federal government to survey the rapidly developing industry of high-explosives production for Britain, France, and Russia. Involved in the production of these high explosives were trinitrotoluene (TNT), smokeless powder, guncotton, and fulminate of mercury. All these substances were made by the action of nitric acid on cellulose and other substances. Lots of nitric acid was needed! All these substances were poisonous to humans. Some work their way into the body through the skin or by breathing in the fumes. All act on the nervous system and damage the blood and body organs. When nitric acid comes upon organic materials such as cotton, wood, etc., it gives off nitrous fumes which exert enough pressure to blow up machinery. During one day's visit to a nitrocellulose plant, Dr. Hamilton saw no less than eight such accidents. The fumes also act on the throat and lungs, and men could get fatal doses without realizing the danger. Doctors, ignorant of these effects, would call it a case of heart failure or heat prostration.

In nitrous fume poisoning, a man would be exposed to the fumes, which made him choke and strangle. In the open air the attack would pass. Thinking nothing had happened, he would go home, eat his supper, and go to bed. He would awaken after some hours with a sense of tightness in his chest and increased difficulty in breathing. His lungs would rapidly fill with fluid, and he would "drown in his own fluid." In milder cases pneumonia or tuberculosis would develop. In the fatal cases the coroner would rule death from "natural causes."

In April 1917 the United States entered the war, and a new interest was taken by the medical profession to protect the munitions workers. Conditions in the munitions plants were shocking, and the manufacturers refused to do anything. The military were indifferent. While protection was available to workers in England and France, there was no protection in the United States. However, the war had a beneficial influence on industrial hygiene. The interest of physicians in industrial poisons was aroused. A change took place in the attitude of employers, too—a large labor turnover was found to be unprofitable. The United States Public Health Service entered the field, and medical journals began to publish articles regularly in this area. Industrial medicine had at last become respectable. Engineers, responding to this new interest, learned how to produce and use dangerous poisons without exposing workers. Removal of poisonous fumes became far more efficient.

In 1919 Alice Hamilton was astonished to be invited to

join the faculty of the Harvard Medical School as a professor of industrial medicine. By that time she was the recognized authority in that field. Harvard was a stronghold of masculinity and did not accept women as students. She had to promise never to use the Harvard Club, which was only for the male faculty; even members' wives were not admitted. She was not to demand her quota of football tickets. When she received her invitation to the commencement, at the bottom of the invitation was written, "Under no circumstances may a woman sit on the platform."

In 1924 Dr. Hamilton received an invitation from the Soviet Union to visit that country and see what it was doing in the field of industrial hygiene. Her friends advised her to join the Quaker groups in Russia because they were "the only foreigners the Russians trust." She arrived there in October 1924 and stayed with Quakers in Moscow. She visited the Institute Obuck, the first hospital in the world devoted only to occupational diseases, with seventy-five beds, five laboratories, and a staff of thirteen physicians. Leningrad and Kharkov had similar institutions. She said on her return, "It seemed to me that there was more industrial hygiene in Russia than industry." The Institute Obuck made routine examinations of groups of workers exposed to certain dangers, and at that time the physicians happened to be working on the men in a rubber factory who handled the solvent benzol. The men would pass the night in the hospital so that all the tests could be made without any interruption of their work. She couldn't help comparing this to a case of benzol poisoning in a city in Massachusetts that had come to her attention. The employer and the company doctor were very secretive, and the hospital had refused to give her any information.

Dr. Hamilton visited Russian tuberculosis dispensaries for patients still able to work. She found the care and facilities "excellent." The patients, men and women, would come during the two-hour midday recess. They were given a nourishing meal and a siesta, well wrapped up, on an open porch. At night they came again for a good meal and a bath, after which they slept in great white bearskin sleeping bags in a ward with open windows.

In a report on her visit, she said, "I looked with a little envy at the women doctors, for never before had I been in a country where men and women in medicine are absolutely equal. The head of the best hospital in Moscow was a tall, blonde woman who had a mixed staff under her. The Medical School was full of girls students . . . some 70 percent of the graduates now are women."

Upon her return from the Soviet Union, Dr. Hamilton reported on her trip at a meeting of the Foreign Policy Association in Boston. In her report, she quoted from the Bible (the Magnificat), "He hath filled the hungry with good things; and the rich he hath sent empty away." For this quotation, she was hissed. "Clearly," she said, "one must not bring communistic sentiments in the Bible to bear on modern life."

Dr. Hamilton's last detailed study of a poisonous trade was made in 1935 at the request of U.S. Secretary of Labor Frances Perkins. An industry new to the United States was using an old poison, carbon disulfide. This chemical was originally used in the rubber industry before it was replaced by harmless materials. It poisoned the nervous system, causing mental disease, loss of vision, and

*Dr. Alice Hamilton*

sometimes paralysis. This chemical now reappeared in a new industry, artificial silk or, as we now call it, viscose rayon.

A serious and rapid outbreak of cases occurred when the rayon industry started and government officials became concerned. Another poison in the making of rayon was hydrogen sulfide, a very powerful choking poison that was given off during the production of rayon. This led to paralysis of the legs and insanity. Doctors knew nothing about this disease, and workers could not claim compensation.

One day Dr. Hamilton received a telegram from an industrial nurse: "Epidemic of insanity has broken out in rayon plant. Doctors do not understand. Can you help?" She answered at once with a full description of carbon disulfide poisoning and an offer of her services. She begged for more detailed information. No answer. She wrote to doctors in the plant and to the nearest insane asylum. No answers. The veil of secrecy had been dropped and was never lifted. She was not allowed to visit the plant, and her efforts to interest state and federal authorities were to no avail.

But Dr. Hamilton did not give up. She secured the help of specialists from the University Medical School in Pennsylvania to make medical examinations. Men were examined secretly without the knowledge of the company and away from the factory. Medical findings were published, resulting in the passage of a law granting compensation for occupational diseases in Pennsylvania. This new law brought about radical reforms in that state and greatly influenced other states. New methods since then have been devised by engineers to prevent the escape of poisonous fumes, routine tests of the air in the plants are made by chemists for amounts of carbon disulfide and hydrogen sulfide, and regular medical examinations of the men are made for early signs of poisoning. Now no large viscose rayon plant is a dangerous place to work in.

On the basis of her contributions to industrial medicine, Dr. Alice Hamilton was an extraordinary woman of her generation. If one considers her involvements with issues concerning the social welfare of women, her status increases to an even greater degree. She studied the employment of women in the dangerous trades, and some of her findings were published in a United States Department of Labor bulletin, *Women Workers and Industrial Poisons*. Lead, which caused the grave danger of plumbism (lead-poisoning) for women and girls, was used in the pottery trade, printing and typefounding, and the production of lithotransfer papers, where women dusted very finely ground lead colors on prepared paper. Solvents like benzol were used in the manufacture of rubber goods and sanitary cans, industries that employed large numbers of women who were exposed to the benzol fumes. Dr. Hamilton found that benzol poisoning was more dangerous for women than for men and especially dangerous for young girls. Chronic benzol poisoning destroys the elements of the blood, causing the victims to suffer not only from a profound anemia but from hemorrhages under the skin as well as from the nose, the gums, the stomach, and the intestines. Women who were poisoned suffered additional loss of blood through excessive menstrual flow. If a woman was pregnant, she could suffer a hemorrhage like that of an abortion.

Thus, an outstanding woman, recognized mainly for her contributions as an industrial physician and crusader

*Dr. Alice Hamilton*

for protective health legislation, can and should be viewed not only as a woman who attained stature in her field of endeavor but also as a woman concerned with, and actively promoting, the well-being of other women.

In 1935 Dr. Hamilton retired and was made professor emeritus by Harvard, and the Alice Hamilton Fund was established at the Harvard School of Public Health in her honor. She left Boston and made her home in Hadlyme, Connecticut, where she spent the rest of her life.

Many honors came to Dr. Alice Hamilton. She was the recipient of the honorary degrees of Doctor of Science from three women's colleges and two universities. She was awarded the National Achievement Award from the Chi Omega Sorority, the Elizabeth Blackwell Award, and the Lasker Award (a United States Public Health Service award; she was the first woman to be so honored). In 1936 Eleanor Roosevelt said of Dr. Hamilton, "I sat there thinking of the thousands and thousands of people in industry who owe their lives and their safety to her, because she had the courage to pioneer in research in industrial medicine."

In her eightieth year Dr. Hamilton was invited by the American Industrial Hygiene Association to give the Cummings Memorial Lecture in Boston. The title of her lecture was "Forty Years in the Poisonous Trades." She warned the younger doctors against too readily accepting statements of employers. She emphasized their need to be on constant watch for old poisons reappearing in new industries.

Dr. Hamilton led a crusade for protective health legislation in occupational diseases when no such laws existed in the United States. Today these laws are found in almost every state in the Union. (As recently as 1971 the

Occupational Health and Safety Administration [OSHA] was created as a branch of the U.S. Department of Labor. It is supposed to regulate the 20,000 chemical compounds used in industry that might harm workers in mills, factories, mines, stores, and offices. Carbon tetrachloride in dry cleaning stores, asbestos in building material factories, and vinyl chloride in plastics plants are under OSHA's supervision.) She fought for world peace, for civil liberties, and for the right to dissent.

A dormitory at Connecticut College in New London was named the Edith and Alice Hamilton House when Dr. Hamilton was ninety-two years old. Edith was a favorite sister who died at the age of ninety-six. Alice Hamilton died in her hundred and first year.

*Dr. Alice Hamilton*

# III

## Dr. Florence Rena Sabin

### Public Health Physician

Considered to be among the world's most distinguished scientists, Dr. Florence R. Sabin's research work on the blood, bone marrow, and tuberculosis won for her the highest recognition of her profession. As a true pioneer, Dr. Sabin's career opened a path for women to follow by including a series of "firsts"—the first woman elected to life membership in the New York Academy of Sciences, the first woman elected to the National Academy of Sciences, the first woman member of the Rockefeller Institute, and the first woman to serve as president of the American Association of Anatomists. Florence Sabin was the moving force in the movement to change the aim of medical study from the *cure* of disease to the *prevention* of disease. Conscious of the important role women have played, she was always quick to point out the significant contributions that women have made and are making in the scientific and other fields.

Florence Sabin was born on November 9, 1871, in Central City, Colorado. Her father, George Kimball Sabin, had intended to become a doctor and had actually studied medicine for two years before he got caught up in the gold rush fever. He left medical school in Vermont and headed for the gold fields in Colorado, but like so many others, he "never made it." In Colorado he met and married Rena Miner, also of Vermont, who had come to teach school in Colorado. Florence's mother died after the birth of her fourth child, and Florence was sent to Chicago to live with her uncle Albert's family. After a short time, she left Chicago and went to live with her grandparents in Vermont, where she attended an academy. She became absorbed in books on science, especially the ones dealing with the way in which the human body functions.

From the Vermont academy Florence went to Smith College, where she majored in science with emphasis on zoology, the study of animals including humans. She was graduated from Smith College in 1893. At that time a new medical school, the Johns Hopkins Medical School, was opened in Baltimore, Maryland. A group of Baltimore women, notably Mary Elizabeth Garrett, had agreed to raise the money to build the new medical school at Johns Hopkins University on the condition that women would be admitted to study there on the same terms as men. This was most important because it was very difficult, if not impossible, for women then to gain entrance to medical schools.

Florence was thrilled at this opportunity to get into a medical school and decided to become a doctor and to spend her life in a profession that she had come to respect and admire. She wrote to her sister Mary of her decision. Her sister was horrified at the idea. "Women just didn't study to be a doctor." Her father was not opposed to the idea but did not have the money to pay for her tuition. Florence, however, was not discouraged. She was deter-

*Dr. Florence Rena Sabin*

31

mined, and she decided to earn enough money for medical school by teaching. For three years she taught school—one year at Wolfe Hall, the school in Denver that she had attended as a young girl, and then as an instructor at Smith College and an assistant in the college library. By the fall of 1897 she had earned enough money, and she entered the fourth class of the Johns Hopkins Medical School, one of fifteen women in a class of forty-two.

One of Florence's teachers at the medical school was the outstanding and well-known anatomist Dr. Franklin Paine Mall, head of the department of anatomy. Dr. Mall was attracted to Florence by her enthusiasm for laboratory work and her accuracy in detail. She became a friend and protégée of Dr. Mall and his wife, Mabel. One day Dr. Mall suggested to Florence that she undertake to make a model of the brain stem of the newborn child, something which had never been done before. Florence was very excited. The famous head of the department of anatomy had entrusted her, a medical student, with a research project! She went to work with all the care and precision that were to be the mark of her work in scientific research. She made a three-dimensional model of the brain that led to a new understanding of the structure of the lower part of the brain. Reproductions of this model are still in use in medical schools all over the world. In 1901 she wrote a laboratory manual to go with her model of the brain—*An Atlas of the Medulla and Mid-brain*—and for many years this manual was considered the most important textbook on the subject.

On June 12, 1900, Florence received her medical degree from Johns Hopkins and remained as an intern at the hospital for one year. When she completed her internship, Dr. Sabin received a scholarship from the Baltimore

Association for the Promotion of University Education of Women and was made a member of the research staff of the department of anatomy. When Dr. Mall died in 1917, Dr. Sabin wrote that she owed "wholly to him" her start in research and her opportunity for a career in scientific medicine.

Dr. Sabin's work on blood began when Dr. Mall suggested that she study the lymphatic system. This is a system made up of very fine, thin-walled vessels or tubes which form around the cells of the body. They then unite to form larger and larger vessels as they make their way to the heart and finally empty into the blood just before the blood enters the heart. These lymphatic vessels carry a colorless fluid called lymph, which brings food and oxygen to every cell in the body and takes away waste products, including carbon dioxide, from every cell. At the time that Dr. Sabin began her research in this area, very little was known about how or where these lymph vessels formed in the body. Using the embryos of pigs obtained from a nearby slaughterhouse, Dr. Sabin made discoveries that overturned the accepted medical theories on the subject. By extremely precise and detailed work, she traced the origin of the lymphatic system and how it developed in these embryos. This was a most significant contribution to an understanding of how the human body functions, and she was awarded a $1,000 prize (a lot of money in those days) by the Naples Table Association for "the best scientific thesis written by a woman embodying new observations and new conclusions based on independent laboratory research." In 1916 she gave the Harvey Memorial Lecture on the subject "The Method and Growth of the Lymphatic System."

With this recognition, Dr. Sabin was invited to join the

*Dr. Florence Rena Sabin*

faculty of Johns Hopkins in 1902 as assistant in anatomy. By 1905 she had become an associate professor, and in 1917 she was appointed a full professor. In the meantime, she continued her research while teaching and included reports of her research in her lectures, making them more interesting as well as meaningful.

Dr. Sabin's research on lymphatics led her to the unsolved problem of how blood vessels—arteries, veins, and capillaries—originate and develop in the body. There followed years of research on this problem, as she worked with chick embryos and other materials. One night, while examining a live chick embryo under the microscope, she saw, as she described it, "the birth of a bloodstream." She saw the blood vessels actually form under her eyes, traced the appearance of the blood cells, and then witnessed the actual beginning of the heartbeat—"The most exciting experience of my life."

As part of her work, Dr. Sabin perfected a technique for a new system of studying the blood corpuscles—red and white. She studied live blood cells by placing drops of blood, freshly drawn, inside a warm box (to keep them alive) and studying their reactions to chemical and other stimuli. She found also that a normal person's white blood corpuscles could vary from 5,000 to 10,000 in a cubic millimeter of blood in the course of a day. By 1919 she had discovered that red and white corpuscles, for the most part, are manufactured in the marrow of the bones. Her work in this area was judged of great importance for the future control of diseases of the blood.

When Dr. Mall, the head of the department of anatomy at Johns Hopkins, died in 1917, Dr. Sabin was next in line for that position, and everybody fully expected her to be appointed to it. But a man was chosen over her for the post. Everybody was amazed. Pupils of Dr. Sabin wrote a petition demanding that she be given the post of head of the anatomy department as was her due. The organization of Baltimore women, who had sponsored the building of the new medical school, let the administration of Johns Hopkins know, in no uncertain terms, of their resentment and anger. The university compromised by giving Dr. Sabin the position of Professor of Histology. This was the first time a woman was appointed a full professor at Hopkins.

Dr. Sabin's outstanding research work and contributions were being recognized all over the world, and her professional prestige was growing. She became the first woman to be elected president of the American Association of Anatomists. She was elected to membership in the highly reputed National Academy of Sciences. Her reputation was worldwide, and in 1925 an important change took place in her life when Dr. Simon Flexner, scientific director of the Rockefeller Institute (now Rockefeller University), invited her to join the staff of the institute in New York City. Thus ended a teaching career of twenty-six years at Hopkins and the beginning of a new phase in her career for the next thirteen years. In a speech before the American Association of Anatomists at the time Dr. Sabin declared, "I have ceased to be a professional teacher, but remain a professional student." She went on to say, "Books are merely records of what other people have thought and observed. . . . The material is a far safer guide." She had never forgotten what Dr. Mall had advised her when she first began to teach: "Never make your directions for students so specific as to rob them of the pleasure of discovering things for themselves." What wonderful advice for all teachers today!

*Dr. Florence Rena Sabin*

*Dr. Florence Rena Sabin*

It was a first for the Rockefeller Institute. Dr. Sabin was the first woman to be invited into full membership in the institute. Assembling a staff of laboratory assistants and technicians, all of whom had the equivalent of a Bachelor of Science degree, she continued her work on the blood and concentrated on its relationship to the specific disease tuberculosis. She had traced down the tubercle, the characteristic structure of tuberculosis in the body, while still at Hopkins. Now she went into a study of the cause of the disease and how it affected the human body. She was convinced that the fight against tuberculosis could be won and spent years of research trying to win that fight. She became associated with the National Tuberculosis Association as a member of its Committee of Medical Research. She was part of a long-term research program in which universities, research institutes, and research divisions of pharmaceutical companies combined their efforts to advance the knowledge of tuberculosis and how to treat and eliminate it.

In 1928 Dr. Sabin was awarded $5,000 by *Pictorial Review* magazine for "the most distinctive contribution made by an American woman to American life in the fields of art, science and letters." In 1929 she was received at the White House by President Herbert Hoover. Of her work at the Rockefeller Institute, Dr. Simon Flexner, head of medical research, called her "the greatest living woman scientist and one of the foremost scientists of all time."

In December 1938, at the age of seventy-three, Dr. Sabin retired from the Rockefeller Institute because of the retirement policy of the institute. She went back to her home state of Colorado to live with her sister in Denver. One would think that by now she had earned a well-

*Dr. Florence Rena Sabin*

deserved rest and would welcome a quiet and relatively inactive life. Not so! Her activities, if anything, increased. As a sort of gesture of recognition to a returning native daughter who had made good, she was appointed to head the Committee on Health of the Colorado State Post-War Planning Committee. It was meant as an honorary title, and no one expected any kind of activity on her part. How wrong that turned out to be!

Dr. Sabin took her appointment very seriously and went into work like a whirlwind. She led the people of the state in a health campaign with excellent results. She went to work on the state legislature and brought in and fought for bills that were enacted into law and stand today as patterns for health legislation everywhere. She actively lobbied among the state legislators, giving them no rest until she got what she was after. She held a banquet for the "milk people" and lectured them on pasteurization. She lectured sanitary engineers on sewage disposal. She succeeded in getting health planks incorporated into both Republican and Democratic party platforms. She distributed leaflets containing health propaganda. She spoke before the League of Women Voters, Chambers of Commerce, church congregations, Parent-Teacher Associations, and other organizations. She rounded up influential citizens to work on health projects such as proper sewage disposal, garbage collection, rat extermination, and restaurant sanitation.

In 1948, at the age of seventy-six, Dr. Sabin began a mass tuberculosis X-ray survey. As a result, within two years Denver's death rate from tuberculosis was cut in half! The National Tuberculosis Association awarded her the Trudeau Medal for "meritorious contribution to the cause, treatment and prevention of tuberculosis." She received the Jane Addams Medal for "untiring achievement in Colorado public health work." In 1952, one year before her death, the Business and Professional Women's Club of Colorado made her an honorary member and established the Sabin Award in Public Health in her name. Colorado could not possibly have known what it had started when it named Dr. Sabin as head of the Committee on Health.

Dr. Sabin had numerous scientific articles published in medical journals and was called upon to speak on a number of occasions on subjects dealing with her research. In 1921 she went to China to deliver an address at the opening of the Peking Union Medical College and while there was awarded a medal. In the same year, at a huge gathering in Carnegie Hall in New York City, Dr. Sabin welcomed Madame Marie Curie, who had come to visit America on behalf of the women of science. In an address at Bryn Mawr College in 1936 entitled "Women in Science," she paid tribute to the early fighters in the cause of women's rights. She spoke of the significant contributions made by women to scientific progress. Dr. Sabin also held honorary degrees from more than a dozen leading universities.

Described as a woman with a "marvelous personality," a kindly face, keen eyes, and a warm smile, Dr. Sabin had visions beyond the confines of her laboratory. She saw the need to apply medical science on a large scale to all people through endowed hospitals, hospitals for group nursing, and group medical insurance. In 1958, five years after her death on October 3, 1953 the United States Congress accepted a statue of Florence R. Sabin presented to it by the state of Colorado.

The aim of Dr. Sabin's life, toward which she devoted

*Dr. Florence Rena Sabin*

all her energies, is best expressed in her own words: "A time will come when men and women will live their allotted span quietly, peacefully, without illness, free from pain, until they pass gently, as a tired child closes sleepy eyes, from this world to the next."

# IV

## Dr. Lise Meitner

### Nuclear Physicist

Very few people know that it was a woman, Dr. Lise Meitner, who introduced the term "nuclear fission" into the scientific vocabulary. Probably fewer know that this woman was the first to recognize that the atom could be split to release tremendous amounts of energy—atomic energy. As a result of her pioneering work, the era of atomic energy was opened, and we now have the nuclear reactor for the production of electricity, the use of radioactive isotopes in medicine and in industry, and unfortunately the development of the horrendous atomic bomb.

Born in Vienna, Austria, on November 7, 1878, Lise Meitner was the daughter of Philipp and Hedwig Meitner. Although both parents were of the Jewish faith, all of their eight children were baptized and brought up as Protestants. Perhaps this was done to protect the children from the anti-Semitism common in those days.

As a student Lise developed an interest in atomic physics from reading newspaper accounts of the discovery of radium by Pierre and Marie Curie in 1902. Intent upon a career in physics, she had entered the University

*Dr. Lise Meitner*

of Vienna in 1901. This had not been so simple as it sounds. It must be remembered that in those days there was a strong feeling among faculty members and students against the presence of a woman in a university. Indeed, a female student then was something of a freak. Not allowing herself to be swayed from her goal, however, Lise went on to graduate from the university in 1906 with a doctorate—one of the first women to do so.

For some time after graduation, Dr. Meitner remained in Vienna and became very interested in the *new* subject of radioactivity. This interest came to be her life's work and led to her opening up the field of atomic energy. But in those days Berlin, not Vienna, was the center of scientific work and progress. The great and famous scientists were there, and they attracted students from all over the world. So it was that in 1908 Lise Meitner went to Berlin to study theory under the world-famous German physicist Dr. Max Planck. (Dr. Planck originated the quantum theory, which was so important to modern physics and for which he was to receive the Nobel Prize in 1918.) Later Dr. Meitner became Dr. Planck's assistant at the University of Berlin, in which capacity she served for three years.

It was while she was working with Dr. Planck that Dr. Meitner met Dr. Otto Hahn, with whom she would collaborate for the next thirty years. He was looking for a physicist to help him in his work on the chemistry of radioactivity. The prejudice of the times, however, made it impossible for a woman to work at the Chemical Institute, where Dr. Hahn was doing his work. Drs. Hahn and Meitner found a carpenter's workshop in a basement where they set up their laboratory. Dr. Hahn, a chemist, was interested in the discovery of new chemical elements and their properties. Dr. Meitner was concerned with the radiations of these new elements. Both did pioneering work in the field of radioactivity.

To understand Dr. Meitner's work and her contributions more easily, it would be well at this point to define some of the terms that have been used and will be used. To begin with, all matter is made up of fundamental units called molecules, which in turn are made up of basic units called atoms. An atom is made up of a center called the nucleus with electrons that move around it. Inside the nucleus are found the protons and neutrons. Protons are particles of matter that are electrically charged with a positive charge. Electrons have a negative charge. Neutrons are neutral particles that are made up of a proton and an electron held together. Other particles are known to exist, but we are not concerned with them at this time.

Certain chemical elements give off particles or rays, thereby changing into other elements. Such elements are called radioactive. Some nineteen elements have this property of giving off particles in nature and are therefore said to be naturally radioactive. Examples of such elements are radium and uranium. Other elements can be made to become radioactive by being bombarded with high-speed atomic particles, as in a nuclear reactor or in a cyclotron. Radioactive elements may give off alpha particles or beta particles or gamma rays or any combination of these. An alpha particle is made up of two protons and two neutrons (the nucleus of the helium atom). A beta particle is an electron that comes from the nucleus of an atom and is the result of a neutron's being split apart into a proton and an electron. A gamma ray is very similar to an X-ray. Alpha particles do not have much penetrating power and can be stopped by a piece of paper. Beta

*Dr. Lise Meitner*

particles are more penetrating but can be stopped by a thin piece of metal such as a sheet of aluminum. Gamma rays are extremely penetrating (even more so than X-rays) and can be stopped only by lead or concrete.

Radioactivity was accidentally discovered in 1896 by Antoine Henri Becquerel of the Sorbonne in France. He gave the process its name. This came shortly after the discovery of X-rays by Wilhelm Roentgen in 1895. These two discoveries, coupled with others like the investigations of J. J. Thomson on the electron and Max Planck on the quantum nature of radiation, introduced the era of modern physics. Great contributions to the development of radioactivity were made by Pierre and Marie Curie, who discovered radium while studying natural radioactive deposits.

Scientists have used alpha particles, gamma rays, neutrons, and protons to change one element into another and thus produce elements artificially. In 1919, for example, Ernest Rutherford, in his laboratory in England, changed nitrogen into oxygen by bombarding it with fast alpha particles (obtained from radium). The following reaction took place:

Nitrogen + alpha particle→ Oxygen + a proton

It was in this way that Rutherford discovered the proton. In 1932 James Chadwick, working in Rutherford's laboratory, discovered the neutron by bombarding the chemical element berylium with alpha particles, changing the berylium into carbon with the giving off of a neutron:

Berylium + alpha particle→ Carbon + neutron

When World War I broke out in 1914, Otto Hahn and Lise Meitner were hot on the trail of a new element. With

Dr. Lise Meitner

the advent of the war, however, Dr. Hahn was called to military service, and Dr. Meitner volunteered as an X-ray nurse with the Austrian army. She was still an Austrian citizen. They continued their collaboration whenever circumstances permitted, and toward the end of the war success crowned their efforts. They were able to announce to the scientific world a new chemical element, which they named protactinium.

In 1918 Dr. Meitner was appointed head of the physics department of the famous Kaiser Wilhelm Institute. She was asked to organize a department of physical radioactivity. There she had excellent research facilities and a staff of assistants and students. She concentrated on the study of the natural and artificial transmutation of the elements—that is, changing one chemical element into a different one by bombarding it with alpha particles, neutrons, and other atomic bullets.

Dr. Meitner continued her work on radioactive elements and published numerous reports of her work. In the 1930s scientists all over the world and especially in Berlin were very interested in and working enthusiastically in the exciting new field of nuclear physics. Extraordinary progress was being made in a short time. The proton and neutron, as well as artificial radioactivity, had already been discovered. In 1934, Drs. Meitner and Hahn again actively collaborated. They were particularly excited about the work of Enrico Fermi in Italy, who was bombarding heavy elements like uranium with neutrons and getting new elements that were *heavier* than uranium, called transuranium elements. They repeated Fermi's experiments to verify his results and succeeded in doing so. Such verification is important if the results are to be accepted by the scientific world.

*Women Pioneers of Science*

One day Drs. Meitner and Hahn were in their laboratory firing slow-speed neutrons at the uranium nucleus, hoping to obtain a new heavier-than-uranium element (a transuranium element). They were amazed and rather puzzled to detect the presence of barium, an element which had not been present before the experiment began. Barium is much lighter in weight than uranium (atomic number refers to the number of protons in the nucleus of an atom while atomic weight includes the number of protons plus neutrons in the nucleus). They had expected to find an element heavier, not lighter, than uranium, and they could not account for their strange results.

It was the great tragedy of Dr. Meitner's life that she was forced to leave Dr. Hahn's laboratory when it was on the verge of perhaps the most far-reaching scientific discovery of the century—the discovery that uranium atoms could be split! With the occupation of Austria by the Nazis, her Austrian citizenship could no longer protect her in Germany. She had never concealed her Jewish origin, and in March 1938, with anti-Semitism reaching a fever pitch in Nazi Germany, Dr. Meitner had to flee. She had already been dismissed from her teaching post at the University of Berlin. She took a train to Holland on the pretext of wanting to spend a week's vacation. She slipped across the Dutch border after a close call with a Nazi patrol. With the help of friends, she got permission to enter Holland without a visa since her Austrian passport was no longer valid under the Nazi occupation. When she left Germany, only Dr. Hahn knew that she would never return.

From Holland Dr. Meitner went to Copenhagen, Denmark, where she stayed for a while with her friend the Nobel Prize winner Niels Bohr and his wife. Soon

*Dr. Lise Meitner*

thereafter she accepted an invitation to work at the new Nobel Institute for Physics in Stockholm, Sweden. Meanwhile, Dr. Hahn, back in Germany, was continuing his experiments bombarding uranium and still getting lighter elements in his results. He was afraid that he was making a mistake in his experiments, and in December 1939 he sent a letter to Lise Meitner in Sweden containing all the details of his experiments for her expert analysis and use. She read the letter over and over and was overwhelmed by its implications. She was convinced by that time that the uranium atom had indeed been *split* with enormous amounts of energy released in the process. She showed the letter to her nephew the physicist Otto Frisch, and both of them undertook to repeat the experiments in order to verify the results. Using the famous Einstein equation, $E = mc^2$, Dr. Meitner calculated that the energy released by bombarding one uranium nucleus with a neutron was 200 million electron volts, or 20 million times the explosive energy of an equal amount of TNT.

In a magazine article describing her work (September 7, 1940), William L. Lawrence wrote, "She was experiencing sensations that must have been akin to those of Columbus. She and Dr. Hahn had accidentally stumbled upon one of the greatest discoveries of the age. They had come upon the trail of what might lead to the shores of the Promised Land of Atomic Energy."

Dr. Meitner and her nephew Otto Frisch sent a report of their findings to the distinguished British journal *Nature* on January 16, 1939. It was published about three weeks later with this historic passage: "It seems therefore possible that the uranium nucleus has only small stability of form and may, after neutron capture, divide itself into two nuclei of roughly equal size. These two nuclei will

repel each other (because they both carry large positive charges) and should gain a total of kinetic energy of about 200 million electron volts." The nuclear age had begun! It was Dr. Meitner who described the splitting of the uranium atom into two smaller and different atoms as *nuclear fission*, thereby adding a very significant phrase to the scientific vocabulary.

When Dr. Meitner informed the Danish physicist Niels Bohr about her findings about the splitting of the atom and the tremendous energy thereby released, he was so excited that he almost missed the boat that was to take him to the United States. There he relayed the news to Enrico Fermi and others at Columbia University. The findings were quickly verified, and the race for the atomic bomb was on.

While Dr. Meitner never thought of the destructive use to which her discovery would be put, and would have opposed it most vigorously, both the Allies and Germany saw the possibility of utilizing it for military purposes. In the United States the War Department undertook the Manhattan Project, under the direction of General Leslie R. Groves, to develop the atomic bomb. In Germany many scientists were put to work toward the same end.

History was made when the first atomic bomb was dropped on the Japanese city of Hiroshima on August 5, 1945. Arguments, pro and con, as to whether the bomb should have been used go on to this day and will probably go on for a long time to come. Dr. Meitner opposed its use and refused, although invited, to have anything to do with its development and did no more work in nuclear fission. In a radio conversation with Mrs. Franklin D. Roosevelt two days after the bombing of Hiroshima, Dr. Meitner said, "I hope that by the coopera-

*Dr. Lise Meitner*

tion of several nations it will be possible to come to better relations between all the nations and to prevent such horrible things as we have had to go through."

The bomb that was dropped on Hiroshima was a uranium bomb that devastated the entire city. The one dropped on Nagasaki shortly after was a plutonium bomb which had also been developed in the Manhattan Project. News of the atomic bomb came as a complete surprise to Dr. Meitner, who said, "I was surprised that it had been perfected in so short a time. It was an unfortunate accident that this discovery came about in time of war." Thereafter she often took pains to dissociate her work from the atomic bomb. "I do not see why everybody is making such a fuss over me," she said in an interview shortly after the war. "I have not designed any atomic bomb. I don't even know what one looks like nor how it works technically. I must stress that I myself have not in any way worked on the smashing of the atom with the idea of producing death-dealing weapons. You must not blame us scientists for the use to which war technicians have put our discoveries." Expressing her hopes for world cooperation and peaceful use of science's tremendous discovery, Dr. Meitner said, "Women have a great responsibility and they are obliged to try so far as they can to prevent another war." She was long a proponent of international cooperation to prevent the destructive use of atomic weapons.

In October 1945 Dr. Meitner was elected a foreign member of the Swedish Academy of Science. This honor had been conferred on only two other women in the 200 years of the academy's existence—a Swedish woman elected in 1748 and Madame Curie elected in 1910.

In 1946 Dr. Meitner came to the United States, where

she was a visiting professor for a year at Catholic University in Washington, D.C. She was a soft-spoken woman with an easy smile who spoke English well but with a heavy accent. After retiring in 1947 at age sixty-nine, she continued to work in a laboratory at the Royal Academy for Engineering Sciences, where a nuclear reactor was being built in cooperation with the Swedish Atomic Energy Committee.

In 1958 Dr. Meitner moved to England to join her nephews and nieces. Her nephew Dr. Otto Frisch by then was chairman of the natural philosophy department at Cambridge University. She continued to travel, lecture, and attend concerts (her love of music was lifelong). However, age began to slow down her activities considerably. In 1966 Dr. Meitner shared the Atomic Energy Commission's $50,000 Enrico Fermi Award with Dr. Hahn and Dr. Fritz Strassman, both former colleagues. She was too frail by then to travel to Vienna to accept the award, so Dr. Glenn T. Seaborg, chairman of the Atomic Energy Commission, traveled to Cambridge, England, to present it to her. Dr. Meitner died in a nursing home on October 27, 1968, just days before her ninetieth birthday. Dr. Otto Hahn, with whom she had been associated in research for thirty years, died in July of the same year, three months before his former colleague.

Why Dr. Lise Meitner never received the Nobel Prize for her pioneering work in opening up the atomic age remains a mystery to many scientists. Many received the prize for a lesser contribution.

*Dr. Lise Meitner*

# V

## Dr. Leta S. Hollingworth

### Educational Psychologist

Pioneer in the science of clinical psychology and world-renowned authority on the psychology and education of exceptional children, Leta Stetter Hollingworth had a career of brilliance and great productivity. An early fighter for women's rights, she successfully challenged the myths of men's superiority over women by her scientific researches.

Leta Stetter was born on May 25, 1886, at Dakota Junction near the town of Chadron, Nebraska. She was the eldest of three daughters of John and Margaret Stetter. Her father was a migrant farmer who also served his community as a preacher. Her ancestors were all pioneers who had played their part in the "winning of the West." She herself was the first white child born in Dawes County, Nebraska, and was brought up in a log cabin. She first attended school in a one-room log schoolhouse, and her earliest memories were of cowboys, longhorn cattle, Indians, army posts, roundups, blizzards, dust storms, and the building of the Northwestern Railroad.

"As a child I saw my grandfather's plow turn miles of prairie that had never been cut before. All my memories are of the 'sod house frontier' where I acquired a splendid set of work habits and all the benefits to be derived from mastering farm animals, blizzards, sand storms and cacti." During her professional career Leta was no less the pioneer and had no less need for ability to withstand new types of blizzards, storms, and cacti.

Leta finished high school in the neighboring town of Valentine and was graduated in a class of six girls and two boys, at the age of sixteen. She went on to the University of Nebraska, where she was elected class poet and graduated with the highest of honors, including election to the honor fraternity Phi Beta Kappa. It was during her sophomore year at the university that she met her future husband, Harry L. Hollingworth. He was attracted to her by her personality and appearance and described her as small and graceful with a lively gait, full of enthusiasm and animation, unpretending and friendly, someone who had a genuine zest for living and an insatiable curiosity.

Upon graduation in 1906 Leta received a state teacher's certificate and secured a teaching position with School District Number 6, in Saline County, Nebraska. As assistant principal of the high school she was paid $60 per month. Her duties, besides teaching, were to "keep the schoolhouse in good repair, to provide the necessary fuel and supplies, and to furnish janitor work." She taught English, Latin, German, history, physiology, civics, and botany.

In the meantime, Harry Hollingworth had gone to Columbia University in New York City after his graduation for graduate work toward a doctor's degree (Ph.D.) in psychology. He got a job as assistant in the psychology department. After teaching in Nebraska for two years,

*Dr. Leta S. Hollingworth*

Leta resigned her teaching position and went to New York City, where she married Harry on December 31, 1908. Harry got his Ph.D. degree in May 1909 and was appointed an instructor of psychology and logic at the salary of $1,000 per year. Life was financially difficult for the newly married couple. Side jobs such as tutoring helped somewhat. Married women were not allowed to teach in the public schools of New York City in those days. Leta, fortunately, was an excellent seamstress, and in the early years her dresses, tailored suits, coats, and hats, as well as some of her husband's shirts, were made at home.

Leta Hollingworth enrolled at Columbia University to study for the master's degree in psychology and was awarded the degree in June 1913. This led to a temporary job administering mental tests (Binet, Goddard, and Terman) in a clinic for mental defectives, and she did very well. The following year all psychological examiners giving mental tests were put under civil scervice supervision, and competitive examinations were given to establish an eligibility list from which appointments were to be made. The first position as psychologist under the civil service in New York was thus established, and Leta Hollingworth, heading the list, was appointed to fill it.

As her first assignment, Leta Hollingworth was sent to the Psychopathic Service at Bellevue Hospital in New York City. The head of the service said to her, "And what do you do?"

She answered, "I am a psychologist."

"And what is that?"

"I give mental tests."

This conversation shows how new mental tests were at

that time and how little those in the professions knew about them.

As a clinical and consulting psychologist at Bellevue, Leta Hollingworth became well known and highly respected. She was skillful and effective in establishing rapport with those with whom she worked, patients or members of the staff. She had a keen sense of scientific precision, and her gift of interpreting her observations and articulating her results made her work as a clinician unusually valuable. Soon cases began to be referred to her by individual physicians and educators, parents, school administrators, and lawyers. She served as psychological adviser, during her lifetime, to at least four or five thousand distressed individuals.

Leta Hollingworth warned her colleagues about superficiality in clinical psychology. She was especially concerned about the kind of group testing that went on. She pointed to the widespread application of hastily constructed group tests to large groups of children who could not be seen individually while they were being tested. She warned that many of the group tests on the market were poorly made, poorly standardized, and of doubtful validity. She cautioned that these ill-advised tests were administered and scored by those who did not know the techniques of testing. She said, "No observation of individuals can be made in group testing. A child who copies the work of his neighbor, the one who is partially deaf and hears instructions imperfectly, the one who sees imperfectly, the one who pauses to scratch his ear—these handicaps, all of which produce unreliabilities in individual scores, are not taken into account in group testing."

Clinical psychology in Leta Hollingworth's days

*Dr. Leta S. Hollingworth*

seemed to be mainly the study of the mentally backward since it was felt that the bright children could take care of themselves. In later years she was to have as her chief interest the gifted individuals, as we shall see.

In June 1916 Leta Hollingworth was awarded the Ph.D. degree. Her doctoral dissertation, *Functional Periodicity*, was a landmark on the psychology of women and a challenge to the theory of male superiority championed by the well-known and influential Columbia educational psychologist Edward L. Thorndike. It will be remembered that at the time women were not allowed to vote, that they could not be appointed to various jobs, and that when they did find work, it was usually for a smaller salary, not because their work was less valuable but simply because they were women.

Dr. Hollingworth's research came across the following reasons said to account for the relative inferiority of women:

1. Women are actually inferior in their abilities to men and should be treated accordingly.
2. Women have just as good abilities as men, but these talents lie all in the direction of sympathy, tenderness, nursing, child care, and the like.
3. Women are primarily and biologically sex objects, and their primary role is and ought to be based on their reproductive function. At most they should merely serve as interesting companions to men.
4. Women, by virtue of the rhythm of their menstrual functions, experience regularly recurring interferences with the use of all their abilities and must be considered for a considerable part of each lunar period as invalids or semi-invalids.

*Women Pioneers of Science*

Dr. Leta S. Hollingworth

5. Women as a species are less variable among themselves than are men. All women are pretty much alike, but men range enormously in their talents.

Leta Hollingworth questioned every one of these myths and submitted them to scientific examination and investigation. She did an experimental study on the mental and motor abilities of men and women for a period of six weeks. Women subjects were asked to make a note of their menstruation during the six-week period. She found no answers, as a result of this experiment, that were attributed to menstruation in the work of the women subjects and found no evidence that there was any variation in performance associated with it. By precise, scientific experimentation she proved that women are not different from men in their abilities. In her experimentation, she used a large number of laboratory measurements of speed, accuracy, and steadiness and covered both motor and more strictly mental activities. Thus, she blasted away the last foothold of the antifeminists—the myth of the inherent greater variability of the male.

Dr. Hollingworth was hailed by the "feminist" group of women in New York as the much needed scientific pillar for the "cause." In the *New York Times Magazine* of September 19, 1915, she was given a full-page write-up under the title "Is Woman Biologically Barred from Success?" She and her husband marched in the women's suffrage parades, and she served as a watcher at the polling places for the Women's Suffrage party. However, she regarded political reform as less important than a reform of attitudes in bringing about a change in the status of women.

When she had received her doctorate, Dr. Hollingworth

was offered a job as instructor in educational psychology at Teachers College, Columbia University. At the time she was working in Bellevue Hospital and had just been offered the position of director of the Psychological Laboratory there. She decided in favor of the educational rather than the clinical field and accepted the Columbia position. Three years later, in 1919, she was promoted to the rank of assistant professor (she became an associate professor in 1923 and a full professor in 1929).

Dr. Hollingworth's first field of specialization was in the area of mental and emotional abnormality. For nearly twenty years she conducted classes in clinical psychology and was coauthor of the important book *The Problem of Mental Disorder*, published in 1934. She also entered the related fields of the psychology of special talents and defects, the psychology and education of intellectually subnormal children, and the psychology and education of gifted children. In each of these areas she quickly got to a position of leadership. Her *Psychology of Subnormal Children* had become a standard textbook upon its publication in 1920. She was responsible for the establishment of special classes for subnormal children in many communities and served as adviser to the officials in charge of this type of education in New York and many cities, states, and foreign nations.

It was in the field of the psychology and education of the gifted child that Dr. Hollingworth worked with the greatest enthusiasm. She arranged with the New York City Board of Education for the selection and education of a group of intellectually gifted children (later known as the IGC classes). She worked with these children from the time the special class was formed, with pupils less than ten years old, for twenty years. *Gifted Children*, pub-

*Dr. Leta S. Hollingworth*

59

lished in 1926, became the standard textbook in schools of education.

To quote Dr. Hollingworth: "Science has already furnished us with a means of identifying exceptional children, and of measuring the amount of their exceptionality so far as intelligence is concerned. If science, within the next fifty years, should furnish us with the means of prophesying adult achievement on the basis of the child's exceptionality, the history of human progress might be modified in ways of which we now can but vaguely guess. We should then be able to select and cherish human genius without regard to race, sex or condition of economic servitude."

In 1937 the New York City Board of Education established an experimental school called the Speyer School (Public School 500) with Dr. Hollingworth as director of research. This special school was established for a five-year period by Teachers College and the New York City Board of Education jointly. It was to be an experimental school for the study of educational problems of exceptional children—the "slow learner" and the "rapid learner," but excluding the mentally deficient. It was here that Dr. Hollingworth compiled the notes and data for her widely quoted book *Children Above 180 I.Q.* Of the nine classes in the experimental school, two were made up of gifted children, while the other seven classes were made up of slow learners.

In her work with gifted children, Dr. Hollingworth developed the concept of an optimum intelligence for total adjustment, a limited range on the intelligence scale between 125 and 155 IQ, and described the social isolation felt by the child who functions at a mental level far above those of his age-group. Other children in his age-group have little, if anything, in common with him mentally, while older children of his intellectual age have nothing in common with him socially. He becomes "neither fish nor fowl."

Dr. Hollingworth's work with exceptional children gave expression to the fundamental traits of her personality and character. Although she despised sentimentality, she was capable of the deepest affection for human beings and intense devotion to human welfare. The subjects of her studies were never human guinea pigs to her. They were the individual objects of her deepest concern. She remained on intimate terms with all the members of her various experimental groups of gifted children, visiting them, encouraging and advising them, and in a great many cases supplying the means for making education possible for them through elementary, high school, college, and even graduate study. She did not want to waste what she considered our natural resources.

In June 1938 Leta Hollingworth and her husband were awarded the honorary degree of Doctor of Laws from their alma mater, the University of Nebraska. From the time she graduated in 1906, she had become a national leader in the field of education. Her books were in use in many colleges, as they were on the campus where she had enrolled for her first course of study in that field. The following year, on November 27, 1939, she died of cancer after an acute illness at the Columbia-Presbyterian Hospital Medical Center in New York City.

In her short but busy and exciting life, Leta Hollingworth found time for activities apart from her professional life. She was an ardent tennis player and played

*Dr. Leta S. Hollingworth*

excellent games of chess and bridge. String quartets and chamber music were her favorites. Not surprisingly, she wrote many poems and stories. In her undergraduate days at college, she had been an English major.

Professionally Dr. Hollingworth wrote four books that were widely published and used as textbooks at colleges and teacher-training institutions. They were: *The Psychology of Subnormal Children* (Macmillan Company, 1920), *Gifted Children* (Macmillan Company, 1926), *The Psychology of the Adolescent* (D. Appleton, 1928), and *Children Above 180 I.Q.* (World Book Company, 1942, completed by her husband). She also had more than eighty articles published in such professional journals as the *Journal of Genetic Psychology*, the *Teachers College Record*, the *Consulting Psychologist*, the *Journal of Educational Sociology*, *Parent's Magazine*, and *Child Study*.

In a letter written by her to the editor of the *Nebraska State Journal* on December 3, 1937, she said, "One more thing I would say. Sometime I shall come back to Nebraska for good. I was born there. I was reared there. I was educated there. I shall take the last long sleep there. The East is too alien for purposes of eternal sleep." In 1939 Leta Hollingworth was buried in the Wyuka Cemetery in Lincoln, Nebraska.

The life of Leta Stetter Hollingworth was characterized by her zest for living, her enthusiasm, friendliness, courage, wit, and understanding. She was known by her friends and colleagues for her quick intelligence, her passion for the beautiful, her devotion to the truth, her remarkable command of verbal expression, and her ideals of integrity and loyalty.

# VI

## Dr. Rachel Fuller Brown

### Biochemist

Rachel Fuller Brown was born in 1898 in Springfield, Massachusetts. The family moved to Webster Groves, Missouri, where Rachel attended elementary school. Her home was near that of a retired high school principal, in his eighties, who enjoyed interesting children in nature, letting them observe wonders through his microscope or watching bees in a glass hive. He gave Rachel a wide-mouthed bottle packed with potassium cyanide in which she killed insects for mounting. Eventually she had a considerable collection of identified specimens, including moths and butterflies. Rachel, of course was properly cautioned about the potassium cyanide, which is a powerful poison, in her bottle. She was warned that what happened to the insects could happen to her. As she recalls, "I still wonder that Professor Onderdonk and my mother trusted me to that extent."

Although this experience captured her interest and imagination at the time, a serious commitment to science came only in her sophomore year at Mount Holyoke College, when Rachel took the required beginner's course in chemistry. Here it was that the experimental method

*Dr. Rachel Fuller Brown*

and exactness of chemistry appealed to her. The chemistry department at Mount Holyoke then, as now, ranked very high. She received the Bachelor of Arts degree from Mount Holyoke College in 1920 with a major in chemistry and a second major in history. The following year she went to the University of Chicago, where she majored in organic chemistry and was awarded the Master of Science degree in 1921.

From the University of Chicago Rachel Brown went to teach chemistry and physics at the Frances Shimer School in Mount Carroll, Illinois. At that time this was a preparatory school and junior college for girls, affiliated with the University of Chicago. Miss Brown taught here from 1921 to 1924. But something was missing. As she put it, "Although I enjoyed the three years there, the situation did not satisfy my intellectual needs as there was no contact with other chemists and no opportunities for investigative activities." She returned to the University of Chicago to work toward a doctorate, which degree she was eventually awarded in 1933, in organic chemistry with a minor in bacteriology. This combination prepared her for her distinguished future career.

In 1926 Rachel Brown went to work as a chemist for the Division of Laboratories and Research of the New York State Department of Health in Albany, New York, where she was to spend the next forty-two years of her productive scientific life. Describing her work there, Dr. Brown says, "I was left pretty much to myself to make contributions to health-related problems at the times when they were currently important." This included work on the chemistry of the pneumonoccus bacteria, the cause of pneumonia, and the standardization of antiserums for the different types of pneumonia. It must be recalled that at that time antibiotics, such as penicillin, which are so successful in the treatment of pneumonia today had not been discovered.

An antibiotic is a chemical substance that is produced by a microscopic organism that has the ability to prevent the growth of, and even to destroy, bacteria and other microscopic organisms. *Fungi* (singular: fungus) is the name of a group of simple plants that contain no green coloring matter (chlorophyll) and therefore cannot make their own food. There are about 250,000 kinds of fungi. They occur everywhere in the water, soil, and air. Some fungi are so small they cannot be seen with the naked eye. Others, such as the giant puffball mushroom, grow to a diameter of more than two feet.

Fungi that live and feed on living plants or animals (including humans) are called parasites. Those that feed on dead or decaying plants or animals are called sapro-phytes. Parasitic fungi are usually very harmful and destroy many useful plants. Examples are the smuts and rusts that grow upon and destroy corn and wheat plants. The Irish potato famine of 1845, which caused a mass exodus from Ireland to the United States, was caused by a mold or fungus. Another fungus caused the blight which, since 1904, has been devastating the chestnut trees of the United States. Other parasitic fungi cause disease in humans and other animals. While most of us are familiar with diseases caused by bacteria, such as pneumonia and tuberculosis, not too many people are aware of wide-spread diseases caused by a fungus. The fact is that there are many fungi (and mold is one form of fungus) that attack and invade the human body. Some cause diseases that are uncomfortable and inconvenient while others cause more serious diseases, some of which may cause

*Dr. Rachel Fuller Brown*

65

death. The control of the growth of fungi is the function of certain bacteria in our bodies. The development of antibiotics in medical practice brought a problem with it. Antibiotics (discovered only in the late 1940s) killed many kinds of bacteria but did not kill fungi; in fact, they often killed the bacteria that were needed for the control of the fungi in the body. When this happened, the fungi multiplied enormously, resulting in a disease called moniliasis. This disease caused a sore mouth in the patient that made eating a nightmare.

Following the discovery of penicillin, widespread and successful searches were made for other antibiotics effective against disease-causing bacteria. Streptomycin, aureomycin, and other antibiotics were effective against diseases unaffected by penicillin. Unfortunately, little attention was given to finding antibiotics that could be used against fungus diseases. None of the antibiotics discovered had any effect on fungus infections. This was particularly unfortunate because with the growing control of bacterial infections, infections caused by fungi were increasing. The problem was rapidly becoming serious.

A research project in mycology, the study of fungi, began shortly after World War II and was carried to successful completion by two women scientists, a chemist and a mycologist. The chemist was, as you may have guessed, Dr. Rachel Brown. The mycologist, Dr. Elizabeth Hazen, also worked for the Division of Laboratories and Research. Dr. Hazen set out to look for an antibiotic that not only would be effective against disease-causing fungi but would, at the same time, be entirely safe to use in the human body. As has been pointed out before, many substances were known to be poisonous to fungi but were also poisonous to humans.

There is a group of microscopic organisms known as the streptomycetes that were known to have antifungal properties, and Dr. Hazen proceeded to isolate some of these from samples of soil collected here and there. When she had selected a few samples that showed promise, Dr. Brown joined her as a chemist to isolate the active principal. The study soon narrowed down to a single organism which Dr. Hazen named *Streptomyces noursei*. From it was extracted the first antibiotic effective against fungi and safe for use in the human body. It was named nystatin after New York State since the discovery was made in the State Health Laboratory. Dr. Hazen carried out the biological studies of nystatin in laboratory animals, while Dr. Brown performed the chemical studies such as the isolation, purification, and chemical characteristics of nystatin. By 1949 the team was able to report a material whose known physical, chemical, and biological properties distinguished it from any of the antibiotics reported by other scientists.

Drs. Brown and Hazen presented their discovery of nystatin at a meeting of the National Academy of Sciences. The publicity and inquiries from drug companies that followed presented a problem as to what their responsibilities were if indeed they had a useful antibiotic. How could they make certain it would be made available to the public? As a result of the investigations of Dr. Gilbert Dalldorf, director of the Division of Laboratories and Research, they turned to Research Corporation, a Foundation for the Advancement of Science and Technology. With its expertise a patent was obtained, and E. R. Squibb

*Dr. Rachel Fuller Brown*

and Sons was granted an exclusive license to manufacture nystatin and to carry out the necessary clinical trials.

The agreement between Drs. Brown and Hazen and the foundation called for one-half of the royalties from nystatin to be made available for the grants program of Research Corporation. The other half was to go into a foundation-administered fund later known as the Brown-Hazen Fund which would make grants in the biological sciences with emphasis on microbiology, immunology, and biochemistry, the areas of scientific interest of the donors. These grants supported the research of individual scientists (often young persons starting their careers) and programs including both research and training.

The first royalties from nystatin were received in 1955, and by 1957 the income had increased to the level where the first grants could be made. Since then more than $6 million have been granted to colleges, universities, and medical schools to support research in the areas of Brown-Hazen Program interest. An equal amount has gone to Research Corporation to help fund its other grants programs. In recent years a large share of the money went toward opening the way to a better understanding of fungus diseases and their treatment, all of which had been neglected. As part of the grants program the Dalldorf Fellowship was established to promote medical mycology—the medical aspects of how fungi affect the human body. The Rachel Brown Fellowship/Scholarship was established at Mount Holyoke College (her alma mater), and the Elizabeth Hazen Scholarship at the Mississippi University for Women.

In addition to being used in the treatment of fungus diseases and infections, nystatin is used to prevent their

Dr. Rachel Fuller Brown

occurrence in patients undergoing long-term treatment with antibacterial drugs who thereby become susceptible to fungus diseases. Some idea of the seriousness of fungus diseases can be gotten from a report issued by the federal government's Center for Disease Control in Atlanta. The report states that fungus diseases of the skin constitute a serious public health problem with untold numbers of people throughout the world being infected by fungi that invade and destroy skin, hair, and nails. An example of such a fungus disease is ringworm, which was so widespread among American troops in Vietnam that in certain areas in wet months it was responsible for more than 40 percent of hospital admissions and up to 80 percent of outpatient visits. The report also speaks of infections of fungi as a well-known occupational hazard for florists, nursery workers, and others who come in contact with sphagnum moss, straw, and wood products. Recently developed skin tests have revealed widespread infections in the general population.

There are other interesting and important applications of nystatin to other than human beings. It is useful in saving American elm trees that are infected with Dutch elm disease—a fungus infection. In the art world a tragic occurrence took place in Italy several years ago, when the Arno River in Florence overflowed its banks. Water got into many of the important art museums and galleries. Nystatin went to the rescue. There was much publicity then about the use of nystatin in the restoration of art treasures that showed fungus growth after water damage by the floods. In laboratories all over the world, tissue culture—the growing of living tissues or cells outside the organism—is a technique widely used in research. Here nystatin plays an important role in preventing the tissue culture media from becoming contaminated and thereby ruined and even helps rid cultures of such a mishap. In food industries nystatin has a role, such as the treatment of bananas, prior to shipping, with the antibiotic to prevent spoilage from fungus growth. Nystatin is also used as a food additive to livestock; in poultry and swine it is used to promote growth and treat fungus infections.

Recognition of Dr. Rachel Brown's outstanding and pioneering contributions to science has come in the form of honors and awards. She received the Squibb Award in Chemotherapy in 1955; the Distinguished Service Award from the New York State Department of Health (1968) "for outstanding achievement in the advancement of health for the people of New York State"; the honorary degree of Doctor of Science from Hobart and William Smith colleges (1969); the Rhoda Benham Award of the Medical Mycological Society of the Americas "for meritorious contributions to medical mycology" (1972); the honorary degree of Doctor of Science from her alma mater, Mount Holyoke College (1972); and the Pioneer Chemist Award of the American Institute of Chemists "for pioneering the discovery of the fungal antibiotic nystatin, which is an important help to physicians and a boon to mankind" (1975). This was the first time the American Institute of Chemists made this award to a woman.

Dr. Brown has held all major offices in the Albany branch of the American Association of University Women. Her nonprofessional activities, when she could spare the time, included hiking, climbing in the Adirondacks, swimming, and golf. Today she enjoys walking, and her current hobby is flower gardening. ("The garden is calling right now!") A religious person, Dr. Brown has

*Dr. Rachel Fuller Brown*

served for many years as Sunday school teacher as well as, at present, member of the vestry in the Episcopal Church.

Asked what advice she would give to a young woman who is interested in a career in science, Dr. Brown had this to say, "If you are interested in science, take more than one science course before deciding on the field in which you want to specialize. Then be sure to broaden your studies with courses in a related field, science or nonscience. Mathematics and English are never amiss. If you qualify for graduate school, make the most of your opportunities. Remember that when employed, you will not be simply repeating what you have done in school laboratories, but you will have skills and trained mental attitudes that can be productively applied elsewhere. Always enjoy what you are doing and believe in the purpose toward which you are striving. It is best not to stick with an unhappy situation or one that has no future. While still in school, a summer job in a laboratory can be very helpful in focusing your objective."

# VII

## Dr. Gladys Anderson Emerson

### Biochemist and Nutritionist

Biochemist and nutritionist, author and lecturer, Gladys Emerson, through her researches with experimental animals, greatly increased our knowledge of vitamins and how they affect the human body. She was the first to isolate vitamin E from wheat-germ oil and study its functions. Her research on the possible relationship of nutrition to cancer and arteriosclerosis (hardening of the arteries) added much to our knowledge of these areas of medicine.

Born in Caldwell, Kansas, on July 1, 1903, Gladys Emerson was an only child. When she was still a baby, the family moved to Fort Worth, Texas, where she attended elementary school. By the time she entered the first grade she could already read, spell, and add and subtract numbers. She recalls the instruction in Texas as being "superb," with instructors teaching their specialties in reading, writing, arithmetic, and music. "I eagerly awaited the start of school each fall. Unruly behavior, vandalism, and lack of grooming did not exist."

When Gladys was in the seventh grade, the family moved to El Reno, Oklahoma (population then about

10,000). She went on to attend the high school at El Reno, where she was permitted to take extra courses in the theory of music, harmony, and counterpoint. Unfortunately only two years of Latin and mathematics were offered at the high school, but her mother "enriched my curriculum in these areas as well as in English and American literature." Her father added to her knowledge of history, geography, and music. In her junior and senior years at high school she was captain of the debating team; that may account for her excellence in public speaking and lecturing later in life. "The high school principal was quite disgusted with me when I insisted on taking the negative side in order to get in the last word." The team won the state championship both years. Two of the topics for debate, that she recalls, was the high cost of living and the closed shop—timely even today.

Of her family life, she recalls: "My parents were the happiest couple I have ever known. They were married for over fifty years without an argument or an unkind word. Our home was filled with friends. They would come for a few days and remain for several weeks. The unemployed and underprivileged in El Reno always knew that they were welcome, and after bacon and eggs, toast and coffee, would work in the garden or in the house. Although my mom was petite and feminine, she was an expert electrician and mechanic. She was an omnivorous reader—president of the Book Club—and the best bridge player in town. My dad was a history and current events buff. He had an absolute pitch and was a 'fiddler' of country music. He and his brothers had a barbershop quartet. As I was an only child, my parents and their friends gave me more than my share of attention."

*Women Pioneers of Science*

Gladys's parents wanted her to be a teacher (so many parents of highly successful women scientists, including those of Nobel Prize winner Dr. Rosalyn Yalow, wanted their daughters to be teachers!), but her difficulty was in finding and specializing in a given discipline. Even at college, she still could not make up her mind between the sciences and the social studies. When she was graduated from the Oklahoma College for Women (now the University of Sciences and Arts of Oklahoma, and coeducational), she was unusual in that she was awarded two degrees, the A.B. degree with specialization in history and English and the B.S. degree with specialization in chemistry and physics—a most unusual combination! Gladys was president of her junior class and president of Student Government in her senior year. Her science career was motivated by three professors at college. It was also influenced by a summer course that she took, while still a sophomore at college, at the University of California in physiological chemistry with Dr. D. B. Hawk, who had written the textbook on that subject that was used in most of the medical schools in the country. This was to become the area of her work for the rest of her life.

Her graduate work began at Stanford University in California, where she was offered assistantships in chemistry and in history. Strangely enough she chose history but managed to include some work in physical chemistry. The year at Stanford was most rewarding, and she received the master's degree in 1926. After completing her work at Stanford, Gladys secured a position as head of the department of history, geography, and citizenship in a junior high school in Oklahoma City. She spent half the time in the superintendent's office working on curriculum in the social studies for the city schools. But she

*Dr. Gladys Anderson Emerson*

realized after some time that this work was not for her.

When the University of California at Berkeley offered Gladys a university fellowship in nutrition and biochemistry, she jumped at the chance and took a leave of absence from the Oklahoma City schools. She was then twenty-three years old. After two years at Berkeley, she resigned her teaching position in Oklahoma City and decided that her future was definitely in science. She taught at the university for three years and then for one year at Iowa State College. She returned to Berkeley to work toward a doctorate (Ph.D.) in animal nutrition and biochemistry. She received the degree in 1932.

Following the completion of her doctoral work, Dr. Emerson went to Germany as a postdoctoral fellow at the University of Göttingen for the year 1932 to 1933. Most of the important work in chemistry in the world was being done there. She studied with Adolf Windaus, professor of chemistry and a Nobel Prize winner. She also studied with Adolph Butenandt, whose work on hormones won the Nobel Prize but who had to decline because the Nazis forbade German scientists from accepting the Nobel Prize. Dr. Emerson describes her stay in Germany as "a devastating experience." The Nazis took control of Germany six months after she arrived, and important scientists and professors in the other disciplines (the "non-Aryans") began to disappear from German universities. From being the center of the scientific world, Germany quickly became the outcast. Dr. Emerson spoke of the "brutality, greed and torture" that she observed while in Germany. "An SS officer threatened to report me for not saluting. I ignored him."

Returning to the United States in 1933, Dr. Emerson took a position as research associate at the Institute of

Experimental Biology of the University of California at Berkeley, where she remained until 1942. It was here that she did her important and pioneering work on vitamin E. The director of the institute, Dr. Herbert M. Evans, had identified and named vitamin E. However, before its properties and uses could be studied, the vitamin had to be isolated in pure form from its sources in nature. Vitamin E is found in abundance in green leaves, such as lettuce, and in cereals, especially in wheat germ. Isolating vitamin E from these sources was a very difficult task but a necessary one if its function was to be determined.

Dr. Emerson joined Dr. Evans in this task, and after three years of research and experimentation, they were the first to succeed in isolating vitamin E from wheat-germ oil, a source rich in the vitamin. They then were able to produce the vitamin in the form of crystals, thereby ensuring that it was in a pure form. Vitamin E is known chemically as tocopherol (*tokos*: childbirth; *phero*: to bear; *ol*: alcohol) because a lack of the vitamin in the diet is known to cause sterility in rats. Emerson and Evans isolated two forms of the vitamin, alpha tocopherol and beta tocopherol. The alpha form was biologically much more active than the beta form. Later alpha tocopherol was also isolated from cottonseed oil and corn oil. Now that the chemical structure of the tocopherols has been determined, alpha tocopherol is synthesized or artificially manufactured in the laboratory and is available as a synthetic product.

The function of vitamin E is still not clear. Although it is required by the rat for normal reproduction, and rats are sterile without it, it is still questionable whether it has a similar function in humans. Dr. Emerson's experiments showed another interesting aspect of the vitamin's func-

*Dr. Gladys Anderson Emerson*

77

Dr. Gladys Anderson Emerson

tions. When she fed rabbits a diet deliberately low in vitamin E content, they showed signs similar to that of muscular dystrophy.

In 1942, at the age of thirty-nine, Dr. Emerson was persuaded by George W. Merck to join the pharmaceutical organization of Merck and Company. She was made head of the department of animal nutrition of the Merck Institute for Therapeutic Research in Rahway, New Jersey. She was to remain with Merck for the next fourteen years. Facilities for research there were much more available than at the university, and there was never any question of enough money to carry on one's research.

At Merck, Dr. Emerson planned and directed researches in the nutritional and pharmaceutical fields and had many highly qualified workers to assist her in the well-equipped laboratory. One of Dr. Emerson's major researches concerned the B complex of vitamins. At one time vitamin B was thought to be a single vitamin, but with further experimentation and research, it was found to be made up of at least seven different vitamins, each having its own function—hence the term "B complex." Her research in this area sought to find out what illnesses or diseases would result when an animal was deliberately deprived of that particular vitamin in its diet. Her findings were made public in numerous published reports.

During World War II, while at Merck, Dr. Emerson did war work in the field of nutrition for the United States Office of Scientific Research and Development and later received a citation from the government for her work.

In addition to her work at Merck, she was appointed research associate at the world famous Sloan-Kettering Institute for Cancer Research in New York City and was

*Dr. Gladys Anderson Emerson*

79

there from 1950 to 1953. She was particularly interested in studying the relationship, if any, between the diet and the growth of cancer tumors. One of her reports on her work in this area is titled "The Effect of Adrenal Cortical Steroids and Diet on Tumor Growth."

Back at Merck, Dr. Emerson experimented with rhesus monkeys, considered closest to humans in their nutritional requirements, to study the effects of certain nutritional factors in producing arteriosclerosis (hardening of the arteries). Fifteen monkeys were fed a special diet, that was lacking in vitamin B6, for from four to fourteen months. She found that the arteries began to harden in as early as four months, and other organs in the body were also affected.

Then, in 1956, came the offer that she could not resist. The University of California at Los Angeles (UCLA) wanted her as professor of nutrition and chairman of the department of home economics. To show how highly it regarded Dr. Emerson, Merck presented UCLA with twenty-nine rhesus monkeys to enable her to continue her research at the university. By 1962, in addition to being professor of nutrition, she had become vice-chairman of the department of public health of UCLA, in which post she served until her retirement in 1970. At UCLA she continued her research on food and vitamin nutrition and published numerous reports in science journals. All in all there were 122 such reports that Dr. Emerson published. She had missed the teaching atmosphere when she was at Merck. As she put it, "The University of California at Berkeley and at Los Angeles gave me the opportunity of working with students."

When asked whether she ever came across any discrimination because of her sex, Dr. Emerson recalls, with amusement, three such instances in her lifetime. "I was a speaker at a symposium on the 'Formed Elements of the Blood' organized by the American Red Cross at Harvard University in 1949. I had difficulty in entering the Harvard Club." Women were not allowed into the Harvard Club, not the wives of faculty members and not even Dr. Alice Hamilton, who was on the faculty of Harvard. The second instance also took place at the Harvard Club, but this time in New York. The occasion was a party honoring the seventieth birthday of Sir Robert Robinson, professor of chemistry at Oxford and Nobel laureate. Dr. Emerson was again refused admission to enter because no women were allowed. "I walked up five or six flights of *back* stairs." The third time was when Merck asked her to speak at a luncheon at the Detroit Athletic Club. "A doorman in livery was so shocked that he pushed the revolving door with such vigor that two guests were forced out behind me. I had to enter a rear door."

In 1943 Dr. Emerson was elected to the Oklahoma Hall of Fame, in 1951 she was named "Woman of the Month" by the American Women's Association, in 1952 she was awarded the Garvan Medal by the American Chemical Society, and in 1959 she received the Certificate Award from the American Association for the Advancement of Science. She represented the United States at international congresses in biological sciences at Rome in 1932, in Zurich in 1938, in Oxford in 1947, in Brussels in 1951, in Vienna in 1958, in Moscow in 1961, in Edinburgh in 1963, and in Hamburg in 1964.

In 1969 Dr. Emerson was appointed by the President of the United States as vice-chairman of the Panel on the Provision of Food as It Affects the Consumer (the White House Conference on Food, Nutrition, and Health). In

*Dr. Gladys Anderson Emerson*

1970 she was an expert witness before the Food and Drug Administration in Washington, D.C., in Hearings on Vitamins and Mineral Supplements and Additives to Food. In February of the same year, she was an invited participant at the National Health Forum held in Washington, D.C. She was an adviser for the National Broadcasting Company on its televised program *Food Facts and Fads.*

More active at seventy-six than most people half her age, Dr. Emerson is a board member of the Southern California Committee of the World Health Organization, is active in the California State Nutrition Council, is a member of the planning committee of the Western USA, Canada and Mexico Economic Conference, is a board member of Meals For Millions (Nutrition Programs Committee), and is on the planning committee for the International Year of the Child in 1979.

In her "spare" time Dr. Emerson has a number of hobbies, such as music, theater, and spectator sports—football, baseball, and basketball. She is an excellent amateur photographer, has a number of cameras and special lenses, and has won a number of prizes in that field. She does her own enlarging of photographs in black and white.

In May 1970 a symposium was held to honor Dr. Gladys Emerson. Among the speakers were Dr. Jean Mayer, the President's Special Consultant on Health and Nutrition, and Dr. Grace Goldsmith, dean of public health at Tulane University.

"If I were a student today," says Dr. Emerson, "I would be an M.D. as well as a Ph.D."

# VIII

## Dr. Maria Goeppert Mayer

*Nuclear Physicist*

"Good! I always wanted to meet a king." It was November 5, 1963, and Maria Mayer had just received a telephone call from Stockholm, Sweden, informing her that she had been awarded the Nobel Prize in physics. Later champagne flowed as her friends and colleagues congratulated her. She was the first woman to win the Nobel Prize in physics since Marie Curie won that award in 1903.

Born on June 28, 1906, in what is now Katowice, Poland (then part of Germany), Maria was the only child of Friedrich and Maria Goeppert. Her father was the sixth generation of professors in his family. Her mother was a schoolteacher who taught French, gave piano lessons, and sang and played beautifully. While Maria was closer to her mother than to her father, she was greatly influenced by her father. "My father was more interesting, you see. He was, after all, a scientist." It was because of him that Maria developed a love for science. He would take her on nature walks, they observed eclipses of the sun and moon, and they collected fossils. When, later in life, Maria began to teach, she would say, "On my father's side

*Dr. Maria Goeppert Mayer*

I am the seventh straight generation of university professors."

In 1910, when Maria was four years old, the family moved to Göttingen, where her father had been appointed professor of pediatrics (medical care of children) at the Göttingen University Medical School. It was a fortunate move for Maria because the physics department of the university was becoming the center of activity for the development of the new or modern physics. Men like Max Born in theoretical physics and James Franck in experimental physics, both to become Nobel Prize winners in the field, were already there. Enrico Fermi, the man most responsible for the later development of the atomic bomb, came to Göttingen to study physics with Max Born and went on to become a Nobel Prize winner. It was an exciting and stimulating environment for Maria.

Maria was an exceptionally good student, and when she attended the public elementary school, she was particularly good at languages and mathematics. In 1921 she entered the Frauenstudium, a private school set up to prepare girls for the entrance examination for admission to Göttingen University. In those days it was very difficult for a girl to be admitted to the university. Maria studied hard and after two years took the entrance examination, passed with flying colors, and was admitted in 1924. She was referred to as "the prettiest girl in Göttingen."

At the university Maria's specialization was mathematics. There was a shortage of mathematics teachers in the high schools for girls, and with widespread unemployment in Germany at the time, the possibility of getting a teaching job in mathematics was good. However, in her third year at the university she came under the influence of Max Born and turned to physics, the area in which she was to spend the rest of her life.

At the time that Maria was a student in the university, the study of physics was exciting and undergoing revolutionary changes. Early scientists thought of the atom as a solid sphere that had a positive electrical charge. In this sphere were embedded—like plums in a plum pudding—negatively charged particles called electrons. The positive charges neutralized the negative charges, making the atom neutral. This theory was overthrown in 1911, when Ernest Rutherford in England performed his famous "scattering" experiment. From this experiment he concluded that an atom has all its positive charge and almost all its mass or weight concentrated in a tiny space at its center, called the nucleus. The space surrounding this nucleus, he said, was empty except for the presence of a number of negatively charged electrons going around the nucleus, like the planets going around the sun.

In 1913 Niels Bohr modified Rutherford's theory by proposing that the electrons of an atom revolved around the nucleus in definite circular orbits or paths, each at a definite distance from the nucleus. Furthermore, the motion of these electrons was not in one plane but in three dimensions, describing a path or shell around the nucleus. For this reason electron orbits are often referred to as shells. By 1932 further experiments indicated the existence of more particles in the atom, in addition to the electrons—namely, the protons and neutrons. This resulted in the following picture of the atom:

1. Atoms are made up of protons and neutrons inside a dense nucleus, surrounded by electrons moving in

*Dr. Maria Goeppert Mayer*

definite shells at relatively great distances from the nucleus.

2. Each electron has a negative charge.
3. Each proton has a positive charge.
4. The neutron is a neutral particle.
5. All atoms are electrically neutral because the number of protons equals the number of electrons.

While these theories helped explain a great deal of what scientists found through their experiments, there were certain areas that could not be satisfactorily explained by them. As a result of further research and experiments by physicists, more changes and modifications were made so that today the atom is seen as having a central, positively charged nucleus containing all its protons and neutrons. Surrounding the nucleus are the atom's electrons, equal in number to the number of protons in the nucleus. However, *no specific orbits or paths are assumed for the electrons* as they move about the nucleus. Instead, the electrons are considered to be distributed around the nucleus in a sort of electron cloud, in which the position of any particular electron is *indefinite*.

In Maria's time, knowledge of the atom, especially of the nucleus, was fairly primitive. Things, however, were happening very quickly, and progress in that new science nuclear physics was being made at a rapid rate. In the 1920s physicists like Enrico Fermi and Robert Oppenheimer, who much later were to pioneer in the development of the atomic bomb, and others were being attracted to the University of Göttingen, where most of the pioneer work in physics was being done.

In the meantime, a young chemist named Joseph

Mayer had finished his graduate work at the University of California in Berkeley and came, in 1928, to do postgraduate work at Göttingen with James Franck. It was customary at that time for graduate students, coming from outside Germany, to stay at the homes of members of the faculty. Joe Mayer became a boarder at the Goeppert home, met Maria there, and fell in love with her. The feeling was mutual, and they were married at the city hall in 1930. The same year Maria completed her doctoral work on an aspect of atomic structure called quantum mechanics, passed her doctoral oral examination, and received her Ph.D. degree (two of the physicists on her examining committee were Max Born and James Franck). The theory of quantum mechanics, developed between 1924 and 1933, involves very complicated mathematics and is useful to physicists in describing the motions of electrons in the atom. Our present concept of the structure of the atom is based on this theory.

Shortly after their marriage, Joe Mayer was offered a position as associate professor of chemistry at Johns Hopkins University in Baltimore, Maryland. In the spring of 1930 the Mayers moved to Baltimore. Because of the nepotism policy of Hopkins, which did not allow the hiring of husband and wife in the same university, Maria Mayer could not get a salaried position at the university. She did, however, do voluntary work there because of her love of science and was given the title of Voluntary Associate. It was in this way that many faculty wives were exploited by colleges and universities. Maria Mayer did get a salary of a few hundred dollars a year for helping a member of the physics department with his German correspondence. She had a chance to do work of her own in a little room in the science building, although no one at

*Dr. Maria Goeppert Mayer*

Hopkins did any work in the field of quantum mechanics; at that time it was strictly a European, not an American, phenomenon.

In 1933 two important events took place in the life of the Mayers: Maria became a citizen of the United States and the mother of a daughter, Marianne.

In April 1933 the racial laws of the Nazis in Germany brought about the firing of some 200 teachers from their posts in German universities. James Franck, a Jew, had to flee Nazi Germany and come, by invitation, to Johns Hopkins University. Max Born, also a Jew, left Germany. Enrico Fermi had fled from Fascist Italy because he hated the regime and because his wife, Laura, was Jewish. Needless to say, many of these refugee scientists were welcomed here in the United States by universities and research institutions. A number of the scientists who later worked on the Manhattan Project to develop the atomic bomb were from among those who had had to flee Nazi Germany. Albert Einstein, a German refugee, by his work on relativity made the development of atomic energy possible. Hitler's racial laws and policy indeed turned out to be a boon to the Allied nations. In the words of one historian, his policies resulted in "the greatest collection of transplanted talent, intellect and scholarship the world has ever seen." Maria Mayer was the treasurer of a group of American and British professors who regularly donated a percentage of their salaries to support exiled German colleagues.

Maria and Joe Mayer gave a series of lectures on statistical mechanics, a branch of physics dealing with the study of molecules and their atomic makeup. This developed into the textbook *Statistical Mechanics*, which became a classic in the field.

In 1938 their second child—a son, Peter—was born. The next year the family moved to New York, where Joe Mayer took a job as associate professor of chemistry at Columbia University. They lived in Leonia, New Jersey, near the Enrico Fermis and the Harold Ureys (another Nobel Prize winner). Urey, who was also at Columbia, arranged for Maria Mayer to lecture to chemistry students.

On January 26, 1939, there took place in Washington, D.C., a most important conference on theoretical physics, at which Niels Bohr announced the discovery of what seemed to be nuclear fission (see Chapter IV on Lise Meitner, page 49) resulting from the bombardment of uranium with neutrons. The military possibilities had become clear, particularly to a small group of physicists centering on Enrico Fermi, Eugene Wigner, Edward Teller, and Victor Weisskopf. These were all European scientists who had found refuge in this country from Nazi and Fascist persecution, and they recognized the war clouds in Europe early. Most of our American-born scientists did not think in political and military terms quite so soon as the spring of 1939. As a result of the conference, Leo Szilard and Wigner conferred with Albert Einstein in July 1939, and the three decided to appeal directly to President Roosevelt. In a letter to the President, dated August 2, 1939, Einstein explained the nature of the problem and the necessity for financial support of the work. In his letter he stated, in part, "In view of this situation, you may think it desirable to have some permanent contact maintained between the Administration and the group of physicists working on chain reactions in America . . . [It] may become possible to set up nuclear chain reactions in a large mass of uranium by

*Dr. Maria Goeppert Mayer*

which vast amounts of power would be generated. Now it appears almost certain that this could be achieved in the immediate future. This new phenomenon would also lead to the construction of bombs, and it is conceivable that extremely powerful bombs of a new type may thus be constructed. A single bomb of this type, carried by a boat or exploded in a port, might very well destroy the whole port together with some of the surrounding territory."

The decision to build an atomic weapon was made on December 6, 1941, the day before Pearl Harbor. The result, as we know, was the Manhattan Project, which was successful in developing two types of atomic bomb: the uranium bomb and the plutonium bomb.

In September 1939 France and England had declared war on Germany. On December 7, 1941, the Japanese bombed Pearl Harbor, and the United States entered the war. The day after Pearl Harbor Maria Mayer got her first salaried teaching position since coming to the United States. She taught mathematics and physics at Sarah Lawrence College in Bronxville, New York, from January 1942 to December 1945. From 1943 to 1944 she was on leave from Sarah Lawrence to do war research at Columbia at Urey's request. It was highly secret research on the SAM project (substitute alloy materials) which was engaged in separating uranium 235 from the more abundant uranium 238. U 235 was fissionable and therefore could be used in making the atomic bomb while U 238 was not fissionable. Maria Mayer had a team of twenty scientists working under her. Her husband, Joe, did his war work at the Aberdeen Proving Grounds in Maryland, where he spent five days a week away from home. He spent a sixth day at Columbia. It was a hectic life for both. A nursemaid took care of Marianne and Peter.

Dr. Maria Goeppert Mayer

In 1942 most of the Columbia group of physicists were moved to the University of Chicago, where what was later known as an atomic pile was constructed in a squash court. It was there that Fermi directed the first self-sustaining chain reaction in the world, using the fissionable U 235. The message of success that went from the University of Chicago to James Conant at Harvard University still maintained secrecy. It said, "The Italian navigator has landed in the New World." And a new world it was—the world of atomic energy! Three years later the atom bomb became a reality.

It was the feeling of most scientists during the war, and Maria Mayer was among them, that an atomic bomb must be developed by the Allies before the Germans made one. However, once the bomb reached completion, the question arose as to whether or not it should be used on Japan. A group of seven scientists, of which James Franck was chairman, who were working on the Manhattan Project sent a report to the Secretary of War on June 11, 1945. The report opposed the atomic bombing of Japan. It stated: "The military advantages and the saving of American lives achieved by the use of atomic bombs against Japan may be outweighed by the ensuring loss of confidence and by a wave of horror and repulsion sweeping over the rest of the world and perhaps even dividing public opinion at home." The report went on to recommend "a demonstration of the new weapon before the eyes of representatives of all the United Nations on the desert or a barren island. If America could say to the world 'You see what sort of weapon we had but did not use. We are ready to renounce its use in the future if other nations join us in this renunciation and agree to the establishment of an efficient international control.'"

Testing of the completed atomic bomb took place at Alamagordo on July 16, 1945. The first atomic bomb ever to be used in the history of mankind was dropped on Hiroshima, Japan on August 6, 1945. It was a uranium bomb. Four days later a plutonium bomb was dropped on Nagasaki. The war ended on August 14, 1945.

In 1946, after the war, Fermi, Urey, Teller, and Joe Mayer were offered jobs at the newly created Institute for Nuclear Studies at the University of Chicago with facilities at the nearby Argonne National Laboratory. Maria Mayer was appointed associate professor and a member of the institute, but with no salary. There was that nepotism again—no hiring of both husband and wife at the same university. She was also senior physicist at the Argonne National Laboratory, where she learned most of her nuclear theory. Here it was that she got the idea for the nuclear shell theory for which she would receive the Nobel Prize.

While a good deal was known by then about the structure of the atom outside the nucleus—the electrons with which the chemists were concerned—little was known about the nucleus itself, and that was what the physicists were concerned with. Maria Mayer had been puzzled for years about the relationship between the stability of certain chemical elements—that is, their ability not to break down or be changed and the number of neutrons in their nucleus. She began to consider a shell model of the nucleus somewhat similar to the accepted model of the electrons shells outside the nucleus of the atom. She knew that electrons traveled in shells around the outside of the nucleus. Could there be something like that going on inside the nucleus with the protons and the neutrons? She set up a system of special numbers, which

*Dr. Maria Goeppert Mayer*

she called magic numbers and which represented the number of protons or the number of neutrons in the nucleus of an atom. These magic numbers were 2, 8, 20, 28, 50, 82, and 126. Elements, she proposed, with these magic numbers of either protons or neutrons were extremely stable as she and other physicists had observed in experiments. As a result of observations and computations, plus a good deal of productive thought, Maria Mayer proposed the nuclear shell theory to explain what was going on in the nucleus of the atom. Her theory stated that protons and neutrons orbited inside the nucleus in certain shells or orbits, much as electrons outside the nucleus orbited in shells. This is a much simplified explanation of her theory which does not go into the many technical details.

In April 1948, after much urging and encouragement from her husband and colleagues, Maria Mayer wrote an article for publication setting forth her shell theory. A fuller and more complete report of her work was published in April 1950. Meanwhile, she became aware that an almost identical theory had been developed in Germany by Dr. Hans D. Jensen of the University of Heidelberg. Instead of being upset or jealous, she welcomed this opportunity to collaborate with Jensen and exchanged frequent correspondence with him. Maria Mayer and Jensen worked together on a book on the shell theory which was published in 1955, *Elementary Theory of Nuclear Shell Structure*. During the war Jensen had been secretly reporting to Niels Bohr on scientific progress in Germany. He had also succeeded in smuggling a number of Jews out of Nazi Germany.

In 1959 came the offer from the University of California of a full professorship for Maria Mayer in physics and another one for her husband, Joe, in chemistry at the new San Diego campus. Harold Urey was already there. Confronted with this offer, the University of Chicago forgot all about its nepotism policy and offered Maria a full professor's salary if she would stay. Too late! In 1960 the Mayers arrived in La Jolla, California, where they acquired a beautiful and spacious home facing the Pacific Ocean. A few weeks after they arrived, tragedy struck. Maria Mayer suffered a stroke that left her left hand and arm almost paralyzed. She was in the hospital for two months. Her recovery would be slow.

On November 5, 1963, Maria Mayer was awakened at four o'clock in the morning by a telephone call from Sweden. It was a newspaper reporter calling to tell her that she and Jensen had just been awarded the Nobel Prize in physics. Congratulations of friends and colleagues poured in, led by President Clark Kerr of the University of California for becoming the twelfth faculty member to win a Nobel Prize. On December 10, 1963, she traveled to Stockholm to receive her share of the Nobel Prize from King Gustav VI Adolf. She was the second woman in history and the first American woman to be so honored in the field of physics. Later Maria Mayer was to say, "To my surprise, winning the prize wasn't half as exciting as doing the work itself. *That* was the fun— seeing it work out!"

Maria Mayer continued her research and teaching and wrote more than a dozen articles on nuclear physics, mostly on problems of shell theory. Throughout the years she was an eager gardener, and her collection of orchids won much admiration. Although her health had been poor for some time, the news of her death on February 20, 1972, at the age of sixty-five, came as a shock to her many

*Dr. Maria Goeppert Mayer*

friends and colleagues. Eugene P. Wigner, who shared the Nobel Prize in physics with Maria Mayer and Jensen, said of her, "Her modesty, unpretentiousness, charming personality and the sincerity of her interest in her subjects of study endeared her to all."

Maria Mayer was the recipient of many honors. In addition to the Nobel Prize, she had half a dozen honorary degrees from colleges and universities, was a member of the National Academy of Sciences, the Academy of Heidelberg, the American Academy of Arts and Sciences, and a fellow of the American Physical Society.

# IX

## Dr. Myra Adele Logan

### Physician and Surgeon

A pioneer in medicine, Dr. Myra A. Logan was the first woman surgeon to operate on the heart in the world's ninth such operation. She was the first black woman to be elected a Fellow of the American College of Surgeons. As an outstanding physician, surgeon, and researcher, she served the Harlem and wider New York City community for more than thirty-five years in a long and distinguished medical career which was brought to an untimely end by her death in 1977.

Myra Logan was born in 1908 in Tuskegee, Alabama, where her father, Warren Logan, was for many years a trustee and treasurer of Tuskegee Institute. He was the first person appointed to the staff by Booker T. Washington when the noted educator joined the institute. Seeing her father, in his nineties, striking out across the campus on his daily five-mile walk, one could understand from whom Myra got her stamina and determination.

As a child Myra went to Children's House, a laboratory school associated with Tuskegee Institute which covered the first seven grades. She then attended Tuskegee High School, from which she was graduated with top honors in

1923. Like her mother, Myra then went to Atlanta University in Atlanta, Georgia, and received her bachelor's degree in 1927. She was valedictorian of her class.

Feeling the lack of opportunity for growth in the South, Myra decided to go to New York City, where she stayed with her sister Ruth Logan Roberts. Mrs. Roberts was working, at the time, on community health problems with the Harlem Tuberculosis and Health Association and helping black nurses who were faced with a lot of discrimination. It was probably her sister's influence that made Myra go into the field of medicine. Her brother Arthur Logan also contributed to her decision. He became a well-known and outstanding surgeon, and his interests in community health earned him a hospital named in his memory—the Arthur R. Logan Memorial Hospital (formerly Knickerbocker Hospital) in New York City—in 1973.

Shortly after coming to New York City, Myra attended Columbia University and received a master's degree in psychology. For a short time she worked on the staff of the Hartford, Connecticut, Young Women's Christian Association. But by then she had definitely decided on a career in medicine. Her opportunity came in 1929, when she won the Walter Gray Crump Scholarship for black women—a $10,000 four-year scholarship at the New York Medical College. Dr. Crump, a leading New York surgeon, was the one white doctor in the United States who was very interested in doing something about the black physician's predicament, his difficulty in getting into medical school and his being denied hospital staff positions after graduation. Dr. Crump led the surgical seminar each spring at Tuskegee. He built a small hospital on Seventh Avenue for black doctors at a time when a black doctor in many places, even with a Ph.D. besides his M.D., could not be a member of the American Medical Association.

Myra received her medical degree (M.D.) from the New York Medical College in 1933. Her medical yearbook, *Fleuroscope,* says of her, "Myra's most notable characteristics are her good nature, personality and warmness of heart. To the accepted rule that no one has a liking for work, her industry makes her appear in the light of an exception. She enjoys the reputation of being always busy about something—None of us have ever seen her idle."

Dr. Logan served her internship and residency in surgery at the Harlem Hospital in New York City under the direction of Dr. Louis T. Wright, who had a great influence on her professional life. For six months she rode in an ambulance on day and night shifts. She was about twenty-five then. "I don't remember once when anyone made a pass at me or was even rude to me," she said. "Now an intern goes into a house with a cop." Several times a week she would deliver a baby in a tenement, in the ambulance, or on the way to the hospital. Before she became engaged in cardiac surgery, she patched up many a stab wound in the heart, then worked like a demon to keep the patient alive. "Today that kind of thing is child's play," she later said. "We have the equipment and the knowledge for complex heart surgery. Why, today if you can't put four new valves in, you're not considered much of a heart surgeon."

Dr. Logan was black, female, and a surgeon, a rare combination even today. On a typical day, during her internship and residency, she could be seen coming home early in the morning, visibly fatigued, after standing all night at the operating table in Harlem Hospital

*Dr. Myra Adele Logan*

doing one emergency operation after another, and all without any payment. In those days, simply to be on the staff was considered an honor. The hospital claimed it was giving you experience. Today the doctors who do the same work receive handsome salaries and fringe benefits. Underlying her quiet outer appearance were a great determination, a dedication to her profession, a willingness to punish her body day after day, month after month, if her work required it.

One of the first surgeons to operate on and repair the heart, Dr. Logan was also the first *woman* surgeon to do so. Her surgery included other areas of the body, and she worked especially with infants and young children. On April 8, 1952, she delivered a lecture on "Acute Intestinal Obstruction in Infants and Children" at the fortieth annual clinic of the John A. Andrew Memorial Hospital of Tuskegee Institute. She did a considerable amount of research on the then new antibiotic aureomycin and other antibiotics and published many professional reports in this area. Because of her outstanding work in surgery, Dr. Logan was elected a Fellow of the American College of Surgeons, the first black woman surgeon to achieve membership in this elite group.

One of Dr. Logan's sources of great pride was that of being one of the original or charter members of the Upper Manhattan Medical Group of the Health Insurance Plan, a pioneer in the practice of group medicine. She had the vision to see the advantages of group practice and for a number of years was the treasurer of the group as well as a practicing member. Until 1970 she had an office at the group headquarters at Amsterdam Avenue and West 152nd Street. Of her group Dr. Logan said, "We practice together because no one doctor knows everything. It's

Dr. Myra Adele Logan

easier and better to have a lab and a radiologist right downstairs or a pediatrician next door." The twenty-six doctors in the group represented all races, all creeds, and an outstanding assortment of medical talent. Her brother Arthur was also a member of the group.

In the 1960s Dr. Logan undertook a very significant study to detect breast tumors in women that could not be detected by the usual physical examination or by the usual X-ray methods. By using a larger and slower X-ray tube, Dr. Logan found she was able to pick up variations in density of tissue that faster X-ray tubes could not. She examined more than 1,000 normal, healthy women and then used the special X-ray tube. "Each set of X-rays gets three opinions by three different doctors," she said. "If we detect a tumor, we take a biopsy. Yes, we have picked up a few that we could not feel." This probably meant that the lives of those women would be saved. Early detection was the key to a cure.

Dr. Logan was a member of the New York State Committee on Discrimination in the administration of Governor Thomas E. Dewey, but in 1944 she and seven other members resigned after the governor disregarded antidiscrimination legislation drafted by the committee.

Charles Alston was a distinguished artist whose paintings and sculptures were exhibited at the Metropolitan Museum, the Museum of Modern Art, and the Whitney Museum. He taught art at the College of the City of New York. Being a good friend of Arthur Logan, he met Dr. Logan through him and fell in love with her. The feeling was mutual, but Dr. Logan's honesty and sense of order and fitness was such that before she would consent to the marriage, she went to see her colleague Dr. George

Cannon. As Dr. Cannon tells it, "When she was getting ready to marry, she came to my office for a chest X-ray. She told me of her contemplated marriage and told me she wanted to be sure her chest was OK, and, to use her words, she didn't want to palm off a sick woman on Spinky. If anything was wrong, there would be no wedding."

There *was* a wedding as planned.

In 1970 Dr. Logan joined the Physical Disability Program of the New York State Workmen's Compensation Board, having retired from her medical practice with the Upper Manhattan Medical Group. She served on the board until several weeks before her death.

In addition to her medical career, Dr. Logan was actively affiliated over a period of years with the New York State Fair Employment Practices Committee, the Planned Parenthood Association, the New York Cancer Committee, the National Medical Association Committee of the National Association for the Advancement of Colored People, the New York State Medical Society, and the New York County Medical Society. She enjoyed reading and attending the theater. She also played the piano beautifully and traveled abroad extensively.

Dr. Logan's circle of family and friends took in many notable and exceptional people. Her niece Mrs. Adele Logan Alexander is the wife of Clifford Alexander, Secretary of the Army. Her sister Louise held a high position in the New York City Board of Education before her death. Her brother Harold is vice-president of Tuskegee Institute. Her brother-in-law Lawrence Winters was an opera singer who was well known in the United States and in Europe and who sang with Metropolitan Opera star Leontyne Price.

*Dr. Myra Adele Logan*

103

Dr. Logan died on January 13, 1977, at Mount Sinai Hospital at the age of sixty-eight. Her death brought to an end a long and distinguished medical career. Charles Alston, her husband, died a few months later. Leontyne Price, who was a good friend of both, sang at a memorial held for them.

A former associate characterized Dr. Logan as an extremely dedicated, able, and humane physician whose personality combined refinement with modesty.

# X

## Dr. Dorothy Crowfoot Hodgkin

### Crystallographer

The newspaper headline read: "Nobel Prize in Chemistry Awarded to Crystallographer." The year was 1964. The winner of the award was Dr. Dorothy Crowfoot Hodgkin, Wolfson Research Professor of the Royal Society of England, Fellow of Somerville College in Oxford, and Chancellor of Bristol University in England.

Dorothy Crowfoot Hodgkin was born in 1910, the daughter of the late J. W. Crowfoot. Her father was a classical scholar and archaeologist. He worked principally in education in Egypt and was the director of education for the Sudan. Later he became director of the British School of Archeology in Jerusalem. Her mother was a learned person but had little formal education beyond a finishing school in Paris, where she studied mostly music and French.

Of her early life Dorothy recalls, "I don't remember very well the small schools at which I started my education. My father and mother were abroad, but I imagine I certainly learned reading, writing, arithmetic, and the rest of it. My first really serious memories concern the year 1919, when my mother came back from

*Dr. Dorothy Crowfoot Hodgkin*

abroad and decided that she needed to get to know her daughters, whom she had left behind in this country in the war [World War I]." Dorothy's mother taught the children such subjects as history and natural history. Dorothy also learned about flowers and birds and learned to recognize and name them. She first came across chemistry at the age of ten when she went to a small private school. It was essentially growing crystals which immediately attracted her. When she was thirteen, her parents decided it would be very interesting for the children to see where they actually worked, which was in Khartoum, the capital of the Sudan. They were away from school for two terms. During that time Dorothy had a rather sketchy education—some mathematics from a friend of the family who was a mathematician, plus visits to scientific laboratories.

Dorothy's father had been to Oxford, and it was somehow expected that she would also go to Oxford. But Oxford required a knowledge of Latin for entrance, and Dorothy had never taken Latin. She hastily undertook a study of the language and then learned that she would also need a second science. With the help of her mother, who was quite an expert in the subject, Dorothy undertook to learn botany. All went well, and she was admitted to Somerville College of Oxford University. Before going off to Oxford, she spent six months with her father, who was carrying out excavations in Transjordan. Looking back, Dr. Hodgkin recently said, "I find myself horrified when I think of children coming up to the university today, how much better prepared they are than I, how did I ever manage from the ignorant state in which I was at the time I first began to work at the university." How well she managed is, of course, history!

*Women Pioneers of Science*

When Dorothy completed her studies at Oxford University in 1932, it was suggested to her that she work with J. D. Bernal (perhaps the leading scientific mind of Great Britain; his field was the structure of matter), who had been newly appointed to start research in X-ray analysis at Cambridge University. In 1931 Bernal had just begun work on a group of chemicals called sterols. It was a wonderful opportunity for Dorothy to work with Bernal, and off she went to Cambridge. She did X-ray analysis on crystals of pepsin and other crystals. This was to prove to be very valuable experience for her later work that was to bring her the Nobel Prize.

At this point Cambridge gave her a small college research grant of 75 pounds for one year. Fortunately her aunt (who had helped her through college) gave her another 200 pounds so that she had 275 pounds to live on for a year in Cambridge—not much to live on! During that year Somerville College at Oxford decided it would like to have Dorothy back as chemistry tutor. Seeing her reluctance to return to Oxford, the college offered her a full-time research fellowship for two years; the first year was to be spent continuing work at Cambridge with Bernal, the second at Oxford. She returned to Oxford in 1934, and the rest of her career revolved around teaching and research there. She would often return to Cambridge during vacation times to work again with Bernal's group. In 1937 she received the degree of Doctor of Philosophy (Ph.D.) from Cambridge University.

Her position at Oxford was that of a college fellow and tutor in chemistry. She was given a small space for her research in a laboratory in the basement of the school's museum—a totally inadequate laboratory. When she married Thomas Hodgkin in 1937, money was a problem.

*Dr. Dorothy Crowfoot Hodgkin*

By 1940 each was earning about 450 pounds a year, but they had to have two homes since for most of their early married years he was lecturing in Stoke-on-Trent while she was at Oxford. By the end of World War II they were deeply in debt. It was then that Dr. Hodgkin realized that most of her male colleagues had parallel university appointments. She promptly asked for a university appointment and shortly thereafter was appointed a university lecturer and demonstrator. The whole family financial situation became more stable from then on.

Dr. Hodgkin was awarded the Nobel Prize in 1964 in recognition of her exceptional skill in determining the structure of important chemical compounds by X-ray techniques, in particular the structure of penicillin and vitamin $B_{12}$.

Vitamin $B_{12}$ is important in the manufacture of red blood cells in the body. When an individual has fewer than the normal number of red blood cells, he or she is said to suffer from anemia. Since red blood cells carry the oxygen so necessary to all cells in the body, anemia can be fatal. Vitamin $B_{12}$ is used in the treatment of pernicious anemia. As little as one-millionth of one gram (there are about 454 grams in 1 pound) of this vitamin per day is effective in the control of this disease.

Penicillin was the first antibiotic to be put to wide use during World War II, and it revolutionized the practice of medicine. Antibiotics are powerful germ-killing substances produced by molds or fungi. Ever since Pasteur discovered bacteria, there was always the hope that some chemical could be found that would kill the bacteria inside the patient without also killing the patient. The first success resulted from an attempt to see whether chemicals that would dye bacteria (so that they could be recognized) could also be used to track them down in the body and kill them. This was the beginning of the first group of drugs, the sulfonamides, originally produced by Gerhard Domagk in 1932.

In 1929 Professor Alexander Fleming, a bacteriologist working in the University of London, noticed a peculiar thing. Some mold had started to grow in a dish in which he was growing bacteria. This was not unusual. However, he noticed that the bacteria in the dish were not able to grow in the area immediately surrounding a bit of the mold. He guessed that the mold was able to produce a chemical substance that had the power of preventing the bacteria from growing. The name of the mold was *Penicillium notatum*. Fleming published his findings, but amazingly nothing happened for the next ten years.

Professor Howard Florey and Dr. Ernst B. Chain of the University of Oxford, perhaps spurred on by the successful use of the sulfa drugs in medicine, decided to make a careful study of the substances that had been reported to kill or prevent the growth of bacteria. They wanted to see whether these substances would also be useful in the treatment of disease. It was then that they came across Fleming's report published ten years earlier. They proceeded to test the bacteria-fighting power of the liquid in which the mold *Penicillium notatum* was growing. They found it to be very effective. Within a few months the new antibiotic, penicillin, was being used in the treatment of patients with diseases caused by bacteria. Within less than a decade, this new antibiotic had become the most valuable of all drugs.

However, little, if anything, was known about the actual structure of the penicillin molecule. Nothing was known as to why it worked. Until the structure could be

*Dr. Dorothy Crowfoot Hodgkin*

109

determined, producing it in the laboratory by artificial means (synthesizing) was out of the question.

At the beginning of World War II, Dr. Hodgkin met Ernst Chain (whom she had known at Cambridge) just after he had made successful tests with penicillin extracts on infected mice. He was extremely excited. "Someday we will have crystals for you," he said. It was in this way that Dr. Hodgkin's interest and research work in penicillin began.

To really understand Dr. Hodgkin's work, let us go back to 1912, when Max von Laue made the discovery that X-rays could be diffracted by crystals. This discovery of Von Laue was as important in its effects as the original discovery of X-rays themselves. It was taken up by Sir William and Sir Lawrence Bragg, father and son, who showed that it could be used to determine the structure of crystals in terms of how the atoms that make up the crystal were arranged. (The structure of the penicillin molecule was first worked out, by Dr. Hodgkin, purely by X-ray methods before it was confirmed by chemical analysis.)

The method used by Dr. Hodgkin is called X-ray diffraction. Try to imagine a large ball suspended on a rope from the ceiling and surrounded on all sides by a circular wall. The wall is painted white so that marks made on it can be easily seen. A small hole is made in the wall at about the height of the ball. Through this hole is shot a series of rubber bullets at the ball. These bullets will hit the ball at various angles and will bounce off (be diffracted) onto the white wall, leaving a mark where they hit the wall. If a large number of rubber bullets is used, a whole series of their marks will leave patterns on

*Dr. Dorothy Crowfoot Hodgkin*

the white wall. From these patterns one can get an idea of the size and shape of the medicine ball.

In a similar manner, chemical molecules, which are made up of atoms, can diffract X-rays that are "shot" at them. The molecules are surrounded by a circular photographic film (similar to the wall in the previous example) so that X-rays diffracted by the atoms that make up the molecule "bounce" onto the film. Photographic film is affected by X-rays. When the film is removed and developed, the pattern formed by the X-rays can be seen and analyzed. This X-ray pattern can tell us not only what atoms make up the molecule but the size of the atoms, their shapes, how they are bound together to form the molecule, and their positions in relation to each other inside the molecule. This information is very important in understanding how these chemicals do their work in the human body.

In 1942 information about the structure of penicillin was necessary for the synthesis of large amounts of the antibiotic needed during World War II. Dr. Hodgkin obtained crystal specimens of penicillin to work with. The chemical information on the structure was not well known at the time. The computing equipment available for making the necessary mathematical calculations was even more inadequate. The structure analysis of penicillin took her about five years to complete. The number of calculations needed to determine the structure of even a relatively small molecule, using X-ray methods, is enormous. Dr. Hodgkin said at the time, "Our computing methods were most primitive." Halfway through the war, however, she managed to get the use of an old IBM card punch machine. This helped considerably, and the analysis of the structure of penicillin was completed and fully described by Dr. Hodgkin in 1949.

Later that year, Dr. Hodgkin began the X-ray analysis of vitamin $B_{12}$. She had obtained the first X-ray photographs of the vitamin in 1948. During the next six years she collected complete three-dimensional data by means of X-ray diffraction. By that time electronic computers were improved enough to carry out the necessary calculations much more rapidly than would otherwise be possible. The crystal structure of the vitamin $B_{12}$ compound was completely solved by 1956. The chemical formula of vitamin $B_{12}$, $C_{63}H_{88}O_{14}N_{14}PCo$, shows that it contains sixty-three atoms of carbon, eighty-eight atoms of hydrogen, fourteen atoms of oxygen, fourteen atoms of nitrogen, one atom of phosphorus, and one atom of cobalt. This, however, does not tell us anything about the shape or structure of this three-dimensional molecule. As a result of Dr. Hodgkin's work, we now know just how these atoms are arranged in the molecule of vitamin $B_{12}$ and therefore much about their activity in the human body.

X-ray analysis is not a simple process of collecting and analyzing diffraction data. It is a matter of the scientist using his knowledge, skill, and imagination against the secrets of nature. Even simple molecules often have crystal structures which are very difficult to solve. Dr. Hodgkin is a wizard at this intellectual unraveling and synthesizing process. She is a person who talks of her work with quiet enthusiasm. Since 1960 she has worked in a pleasant modern wing of the chemistry building at Oxford, unlike the crude laboratory assigned to her earlier. At least one-third of the members of this laborato-

*Dr. Dorothy Crowfoot Hodgkin*

ry are young women who are intensely interested in becoming crystallographers.

At present Dr. Hodgkin is interested in and working on determining the exact structure of the insulin molecule by X-ray techniques. Insulin is the chemical involved in the widespread disease known as diabetes. Here the X-ray evidence is important in finding out the molecular structure of insulin and attempting to relate this to its activity in the body.

Dr. Hodgkin is the third woman to win the Nobel Prize in chemistry. The other women were Marie Curie in 1911 (who also shared the Nobel Prize in physics with her husband, Pierre, in 1903), and her daughter, Irène Joliot-Curie, who shared the prize in 1935 with her husband Frédéric. When the award was announced, Dr. Hodgkin was in Ghana with her husband, Thomas, who was then director of the Institute of African Studies at the University of Ghana. Dr. Hodgkin made two scientific reputations for herself, one under her maiden name and one under her married name. Several chemists were amazed to find that the Crowfoot of penicillin fame and the Hodgkin of vitamin $B_{12}$ fame were the same person.

What does Dr. Hodgkin think of the role women can play in the sciences? She recalls, "When I came back to Oxford in 1934, I became gradually conscious that as a woman I was out of certain parts of Oxford scientific life." She goes on to say, "At present the major problem still seems to be that of time in relation to one's career; having children takes considerable time off from scientific work, and young women with families may have to work shorter hours and make, for a time, slower progress than young men." She suggests part-time jobs that can turn later into full-time jobs. She feels that there is still prejudice against women in some circles, and the fact that there are so very few women scientists in senior positions may be due to history and "a slowness in changing our way of thinking and living."

Dr. Hodgkin has traveled extensively to attend conferences and give lectures. She has visited China three times and North Vietnam twice. She is the author of many publications on the X-ray crystallographic analysis of the structure of chemical molecules and compounds.

In addition to the Nobel Prize, Dr. Hodgkin has received a lot of recognition for her work both at home and overseas. She was made a Fellow of the Royal Society of England in 1947, a Foreign Member of the Royal Netherlands Academy of Science and Letters in 1956 and of the American Academy of Arts and Sciences in 1958, a Fellow of the Australian Academy of Science (the first woman to be elected) in 1968, and a Foreign Member of the USSR Academy of Sciences in 1976. She was awarded the Royal Medal of the Royal Society of England in 1956 and the Order of Merit in 1965. She holds a number of honorary degrees, including those of Honorary D.Sc. (Doctor of Science) at the universities of Leeds, Manchester, and Cambridge. She was president of the International Union of Crystallography from 1972 to 1975.

As mentioned earlier, she is married to Thomas Hodgkin, lecturer and author and Emeritus Fellow of Balliol College in Oxford. They have two sons and a daughter. Luke teaches mathematics in Algiers, Elizabeth teaches in a girls' school, and Toby is a social worker in India. Luke has three children, making Dorothy Hodgkin a grandmother. Since Alan Hodgkin, who received the Nobel

*Dr. Dorothy Crowfoot Hodgkin*

Prize in physiology and medicine in 1963, is Thomas's cousin, these grandchildren now have a Nobel laureate on each side of the family.

Grandma Dorothy is still actively at work in her research laboratory and is a source of help and inspiration to those fortunate enough to work with her in the wonderful field of crystallography.

# XI

---

## *Dr. Jane C. Wright*

---

### *Physician and Chemotherapist*

"I want to see a time in this country when a woman in medicine is not such an outstanding exception. I want to see a time when everyone with a bent for medicine is in the field, contributing to better health care for all of us. I want to see a time when people with special talent, whatever their sex, take their place in making the world free of disease." The speaker is Dr. Jane C. Wright, who, on July 1, 1967, became the first black woman to be appointed to a high post in medical administration— associate dean and professor of surgery at the New York Medical College in New York City.

Dr. Wright's outstanding and pioneering work in cancer chemotherapy research carries on the remarkable record of medical service made by her distinguished family. Her father, the late Dr. Louis T. Wright, an eminent surgeon, cancer researcher, and civil rights leader, was one of the first black graduates of the Harvard Medical School. At his class's twenty-fifth reunion he was voted the man in the class who had contributed the most to medical knowledge. He was the first Black to become a police surgeon in New York City and the first

*Dr. Jane C. Wright*

black physician ever appointed to the staff of a New York City hospital. Jane's paternal grandfather was one of the first graduates of Meharry Medical College, which was established to offer ex-slaves professional training. A stepuncle, the late Dr. Harold West, was the president of Meharry. A stepgrandfather, Dr. William Penn, was the first black to earn the M.D. degree at the Yale University Medical School. Dr. Wright's younger sister, Dr. Barbara P. Wright, is also a physician and a specialist in industrial medicine.

Jane Cooke Wright was born in New York City on November 30, 1919, the daughter of Dr. Louis T. Wright and Corinne Cooke Wright, a former teacher in the New York City schools. Jane attended Ethical Culture, an elementary school, and its affiliated upper school, Fieldston. She was graduated in 1938 and entered Smith College. When asked what influenced her to go into medicine, she replied, "When I was at Smith as a student, little did I know that at the end of my sophomore year I would have to select a major, and I couldn't decide whether to major in art or in something else." For a while, she had thought of becoming a painter, but her father discouraged her because "art offered an impractical and uncertain future." She then changed her major to premed. Her record at Smith, from which she was graduated with a B.A. degree in 1942, won her a four-year scholarship to the New York Medical College.

In medical school, Jane was elected vice-president of her class, president of the honor society, and literary editor of the yearbook. In June 1945 she was awarded the M.D. degree with honors. She interned at Bellevue Hospital, where her supervisor rated her as "by all odds the most promising intern I ever had working with me."

She then served as assistant resident in internal medicine from April through December 1946. This was followed by a year's residency, in 1947, and a chief residency, in 1948, in internal medicine at Harlem Hospital.

After completing her residency at Harlem Hospital, Dr. Wright went into general practice and the same year married David D. Jones, a lawyer. Mr. Jones was the executive director of Harlem Teams for Self-Help, an antipoverty agency. Later he served as director of Job Orientation in Neighborhoods (JOIN) for N.Y.C. He was deputy commissioner of the New York City Department of Correction. In August 1972 he joined Syracuse University as vice-president for affirmative action to help develop equal opportunity programs on campus. In 1976 Mr. Jones experienced a severe heart attack and died at the age of fifty-eight. At the time of his death, Jones was a member of Governor Hugh Carey's task force on higher education.

"In 1949 my father gave me a job as a clinician at his cancer research foundation, and I found the work a great challenge." Thus began Dr. Wright's involvement in cancer chemotherapy research, which continues to the present day and has brought her national and international recognition and fame. In her experimental research, Dr. Wright tries out new drugs to see their effects on cancer cells in the test tube and in animals and, if results warrant it, on human cancers. The drugs that prove to be effective are then made available to doctors to treat patients who have cancer.

After the death of her father in 1952, Dr. Jane Wright became director of the Harlem Hospital Cancer Research Foundation. In 1955 she moved to New York University, where she was named associate professor of research surgery at the School of Medicine and director of cancer chemotherapy at the Medical Center. She is a brilliant researcher and a demon for work.

Her pursuit of cancer studies was definitely a result of her father's work. "The idea of cancer research hadn't crossed my mind until I began working for my father at Harlem Hospital. I was preparing for an eventual private practice as an internist. But I became fascinated by the challenge of the job. So much is unknown in the field that there is a constant sense of adventure in my work. I like to think that I am making some contribution to solving a tough problem."

During the period February 18 through March 8, 1961, Dr. Wright had an unusual and fascinating experience. She went on a medical safari sponsored by the African Research Foundation. The purpose of the foundation is to work in cooperation with local governments and people in Africa to provide important medical essentials in areas in Africa where these are needed and wanted. A mobile medical unit—a hospital on wheels—fully equipped with medical-surgical supplies, X-rays, electricity, running water, etc., served as an operating room, clinic, school, and laboratory on the safari. A Land Rover and car accompanied the unit to carry personnel, food, and camp equipment. The personnel consisted of four physicians (including Dr. Wright), one nurse, one laboratory technician, one medical assistant, two interpreters, one photographer, one driver, and one cook. During the week on the safari in Kenya (Masai Land) 341 patients were treated in the mobile unit, individual health instruction was given to the patients, laboratory studies were performed when necessary, medicines were administered as needed, and food supplements were given to the severely undernourished children. In the vast area that was covered, only one doctor was seen.

Dr. Wright and other members of the safari became acutely aware that this sort of mobile medicine must be a regular scheduled procedure to be of real service. In her report, Dr. Wright concluded, "My first-hand experience in the field has convinced me that the African Research Foundation is accomplishing right now a great work at amazingly low cost. What they could do with more support is a thrilling prospect."

In the midst of a busy schedule, she found time to respond to a call from the White House and served on the President's Commission on Heart Disease, Cancer and Stroke, under both Presidents Kennedy and Johnson. The purpose of the commission was to draw up a "national program to conquer" these three diseases. The commission drew up its recommendations, but as with so many recommendations, little has been done about them despite their importance.

On July 1, 1967, history was made. Dr. Jane Wright became the first black woman physician to attain the high position of associate dean of a medical school—the New York Medical College. "Coming back to my alma mater . . . gave me a marvelous feeling. It's like a homecoming." Her duties included administration of the medical school and the development of a program to study cancer, heart disease, and stroke. She directs the cancer research laboratory at the college, where researchers have been investigating the effect of anticancer drugs on cancer cells.

Dr. Wright points out that if our present knowledge about cancer were used on the entire population, "fifty percent of the people who develop cancer could be

*Dr. Jane C. Wright*

121

*Dr. Jane C. Wright*

cured." But the cost of training personnel and providing annual examinations with chest X-rays for everyone was considered prohibitive. "The money made available for cancer research by the federal government amounts to some $176,000,000 a year," she said. "Contrast this to the $553,000,000 spent each year by people on chewing gum. If we can afford these things, why can't we put enough money and enough people to work to solve the cancer problem?"

Being a woman and a black has not been a handicap. Dr. Wright says, "I don't think I was discriminated against for either reason—although I may have been too stupid to recognize it." She does recall, however, when "a bewildered doorman tried to make me take the service elevator to a dinner being given in my honor." She also recalls an incident that happened when she was director of cancer chemotherapy research at the New York University Medical Center. She was looking for a secretary, and the man in charge of personnel telephoned to tell her that he had found one, adding, "It's a man." She remembers, "I guess I was shocked. I told him, 'I can't have a male secretary.'" He was a southerner, and he drawled, "Dr. Wright, don't tell me you discriminate." We were friends, and I had to laugh. I hired the man, and he turned out to be the best secretary I've ever had. He was so good, in fact, that he is now a key coordinator at the university. What's more, we're good friends."

According to Dr. Wright, there are more than one hundred kinds of cancer, and whether they are all caused by the same factor is not clearly understood at the present time. Says she, "I believe the virus theory [that cancer is caused by a virus or viruses] is a good one, and I wouldn't be the least surprised if someone establishes firmly that

*Dr. Jane C. Wright*

human tumors are caused by viruses . . . many people in cancer research believe this."

In the treatment of cancer, chemotherapy is usually the last resort after patients have been to their surgeons and through radiation therapy and have not been helped. In chemotherapy, various drugs are used to try to kill or arrest the development of the cancer cells. The treatment is not always successful. However, there are some bright spots. Dr. Wright says, "I have seen 'miracle' cures by chemotherapy, which was unknown thirty years ago. One of our patients, a doctor's wife, had melanomas, hundreds of small tumors, on one extremity from her thigh to her toes. A surgeon wanted to amputate, but she refused. Under chemotherapy the tumors vanished, and she is living and well seven years later." She goes on to say, "Chemotherapy can be depressing if you don't see success—and I must say there are many failures. But I have seen tumors vanish . . . and the patients are so happy and I am so happy . . . it's so rewarding."

When asked by the writer to compare the effectiveness of cancer chemotherapy now, compared to ten years ago, Dr. Wright replied, "I think that each year since I've been in the field, and I've been at this more than twenty-five years, there has been progress made. Each year or so we have another new wonderful drug or two to work with that does something in another form of cancer. And now that people are using all kinds of combinations, we're getting better and better results. But we still need to look for more superior drugs." As for her research, she says, "There is always this tremendous challenge—nobody else has found the answer; maybe I will."

In her chosen field, Dr. Wright's success has brought her numerous honors, including honorary doctorates from the Women's Medical College of Pennsylvania and Denison University; the Spirit of Achievement Award from the Albert Einstein School of Medicine; distinguished service awards from the National Council of Negro Women; the Outstanding Services in Medicine Award from the Grace Congregational Church; the Golden Plate Award from the American Academy of Achievement; the American Association for Cancer Research salute for important contributions to research in clinical cancer chemotherapy. This last award was made in honor of the International Year of Women, 1975, and Dr. Wright says, "This is my most treasured honor."

Dr. Wright is a member of the Manhattan Council, State Commission for Human Rights, serves on the editorial board of the journal of the National Medical Association, and is vice-president of the African Research Foundation. Beginning with 1950, Dr. Wright has had more than one hundred professional articles on cancer chemotherapy published in various professional journals which reflect the scope of her professional activities.

As for hobbies, she has little time for them these days. "I'm a mystery story fan," she says, "but keeping up with scientific reading leaves me no time for that. I also used to dance, ski, knit, and paint."

In private life Dr. Jane C. Wright is Mrs. David D. Jones and has two grown daughters—Jane and Alison. Dr. Wright says that she could not have got along without her mother, the youthful eighty-six-year-old Mrs. Corinne Wright, in the early years of her marriage when her children were young. "I had a live-in housekeeper while the girls were little—but trying to find one!" She laughs ruefully and throws up her hands. "One year I hired seven women and fired the seven. My mother filled in.

*Dr. Jane C. Wright*

125

Without her, I wouldn't have been able to practice." When the children were twelve or thirteen, she had a housekeeper who came in days to take care of the apartment and do the everyday cooking. Dr. Wright enjoys gourmet cooking, especially experimenting with exotic dishes such as roast duckling with fruit sauce.

Dr. Wright feels that women face certain obstacles in entering the medical profession. "A woman receives a medical degree at about the time she is twenty-six years old, her prime childbearing period. How can she resolve the conflict between maternal responsibilities and the demands of a career in medicine? In the past, doctors who were also mothers either stopped working for a while or employed housekeepers to whom they entrusted the major upbringing of their babies. An intern or resident is on duty twelve hours a day, every other night, and every other weekend, for one, two, or more years. That is an extremely long period for mother and child to be separated. Fortunately some changes are being made, and some solutions to this problem have been provided. Harvard Medical School, for example, has recognized the problems of women doctors and permits them to complete the one-year internship in two years. The department of psychiatry at New York Medical College has changed the working times for its mother residents to spread over a four-year period rather than the usual three years. They also receive a maximum of three months off each year for their family, taken whenever they wish. If an emergency arises at home, a change of schedule may be arranged. In such emergencies, women usually cover assignments for each other. I am happy to say that these accommodations have enabled one woman with eleven children to complete her training."

*Women Pioneers of Science*

A vivacious woman with an infectious laugh, Dr. Wright inspires her colleagues with her vitality and exuberance. She is a dynamic, highly intelligent, and articulate woman who has an insatiable curiosity not only about her field of science but about the world around her.

In a speech to young women she said, "I am one of those women who has had the creative joys of a medical career. I have also had the joys of a family. I cannot think of a better way of life. Because of the challenges, the rewards, and the opportunities for a full and productive future, I would like to urge you to consider medicine as a career for you."

*Dr. Jane C. Wright*

# XII

---

## Dr. Rosalyn S. Yalow

---

*Nuclear Physicist in Medicine*

In 1977 Rosalyn Yalow became the second woman ever to win a Nobel Prize in medicine and only the sixth woman to win that prize in any science category. Only the year before, she had become the first woman, and the first nuclear physicist, to win an Albert Lasker Basic Medical Research Award for her role in discovering and developing *radioimmunoassay*, a new and revolutionary method for the precise measurement of substances in the blood such as drugs, hormones, viruses, vitamins, enzymes, and others. Her new method made it possible, for the first time, exactly to measure these substances in the blood and body tissues which were present in such tiny amounts that there was no way of measuring them before. As the Nobel citation said, in part, "It opened new vistas within biological and medical research."

Rosalyn Yalow was born in New York City on July 19, 1921. Her mother, Clara Zipper Sussman, came to the United States from Germany at the age of four. Her father, the late Simon Sussman, was born on the Lower East Side of New York City, where he ran a small paper and twine business. Neither parent had had the opportunity of going beyond elementary school. Their daughter more than made up for that. Rosalyn was an early reader, reading even before kindergarten. By the seventh grade she was committed to mathematics. At Walton High School one of her teachers interested her greatly in the study of chemistry. However, when she went to Hunter College (now of the City University of New York), her interest changed to physics under the influence of two of her physics teachers there.

In the late 1930s, when Rosalyn was a student in college, the most exciting field was physics, and nuclear physics in particular. Nuclear physics was in its infancy, and extremely exciting work was being done by Enrico Fermi, Lise Meitner, Otto Hahn, and others that would usher in the age of atomic energy. Eve Curie had just published the biography of her mother, Madame Marie Curie, which inspired Rosalyn greatly. When she was a junior at college, Rosalyn listened to Fermi give a very stimulating lecture at Columbia University on nuclear fission, which had just been discovered.

Rosalyn became determined to prepare for a career in physics. Her parents thought she would be better off as an elementary school teacher, but her physics professors encouraged her to persist. She was graduated from Hunter College in January 1941 at the age of nineteen and one-half with a *magna cum laude* and election to the Phi Beta Kappa honor society. As she was ending her senior year, she was offered what seemed like a good opportunity. One of her physics professors, Dr. Jerrold Zacharias, obtained a part-time job for her as secretary to Dr. Rudolf Schoenheimer, a leading biochemist at Columbia University's medical school. This position was supposed to provide an entrée for her into graduate courses, via the

*Dr. Rosalyn S. Yalow*

129

back door, but she had to agree to study stenography. Upon graduation, she went to business school, but fortunately she did not have to stay there too long.

In the middle of February 1941 she received an offer of a teaching assistantship in physics at the University of Illinois's College of Engineering, the most prestigious of the schools to which she had applied. It was an achievement beyond belief. She tore up her stenography books, stayed on as secretary until June, and during the summer took two physics courses at New York University. In September 1941 she went to the University of Illinois.

At the first meeting of the faculty of the College of Engineering she discovered that she was the only woman among its 400 members. The dean of the faculty congratulated her on her achievement and told her that she was the first woman there since 1917. Could it have been that the draft of young men into the armed forces at the time made her entrance into graduate school possible? On the first day of graduate school she met Aaron Yalow, who was also beginning graduate study in physics and who, in 1943, was to become her husband.

The first year was very difficult. From junior high school through Hunter College, she had never had boys in her classes except for a thermodynamics course, which she took at City College at night, and the two summer courses at New York University. Hunter had offered a physics major for the first time in September 1940, when she was already a senior. As a result, her course work in physics had been much less than that of the other first-year graduate students. Therefore, in addition to taking three graduate courses and being a half-time assistant teaching the freshman course in physics, she sat in on two undergraduate courses without credit. Like most first-year teaching assistants, she had never taught before. But unlike the others, she undertook to observe in the classroom of a young instructor who had an excellent reputation so that she could learn how it should be done.

She was delighted when she received As in two of the three graduate courses she was taking. In the third course, optics, she received an A in the lecture half of the course and an A minus in the laboratory part. When the chairman of the physics department looked at this splendid record, his only comment was: "That A minus confirms that women do not do well at laboratory work."

The bombing of Pearl Harbor by the Japanese on December 7, 1941, brought the United States into the war. The physics department at Illinois University was seriously hurt by the loss of junior and senior faculty to secret scientific work for the government. The campus was filled with young army and navy students sent by their respective services for training. There was a heavy teaching load for Rosalyn, graduate courses to be taken, an experimental doctoral thesis requiring long hours in the laboratory to be completed. Her thesis director was Dr. Maurice Goldhaber, who later became director of Brookhaven National Laboratory. He and his wife were very encouraging and supportive in Rosalyn's work. His wife, Dr. Gertrude Goldhaber, was a distinguished physicist in her own right but had no position at the university because of rules which forbade the hiring of both husband and wife at the same university. It was the same kind of nepotism rules that had prevented Nobel Prize winner Maria Mayer from being employed by Columbia University when her husband was teaching there and again at the University of Chicago. Gerty Cori, another Nobel Prize winner, suffered in the same way when her

*Dr. Rosalyn S. Yalow*

131

husband went to Washington University in St. Louis. She was lucky to get a research assistantship at the same time that her husband was made a full professor.

In the meantime, Rosalyn was seeing a lot of Aaron Yalow, the fellow graduate student in physics and the son of a Syracuse rabbi. They were married in 1943. In January 1945 Rosalyn received her Ph.D. degree in nuclear physics. After that, she returned to New York City without her husband since completion of his doctoral thesis was delayed, and she did not want to miss any opportunities in New York. She secured a position as assistant engineer at the Federal Telecommunications Laboratory, a research laboratory for the International Telephone & Telegraph Company, where she was the only woman engineer. When the research group in which she was working left New York in 1946, Dr. Yalow returned to Hunter College to teach physics to a group of veterans in a pre-engineering program.

By September 1945 Aaron Yalow had received his Ph.D. degree and returned to New York to rejoin his wife. They set up a home first in an apartment in Manhattan, then in a small house in the Bronx. By this time Aaron Yalow was in medical physics at Montefiore Hospital in the Bronx. Through him, Rosalyn Yalow met Dr. Edith Quimby, a leading medical physicist at Columbia's medical school. (Edith Quimby helped create the new field of scientific work known as radiation physics. She had much to do with the safe and effective use of X-rays and radium in the treatment of disease by applying the laws of physics to the use of X-rays and radium on human beings. She has written on the subject and has taught many of the physicians who became specialists in radiology.)

Rosalyn Yalow volunteered to work in Dr. Quimby's laboratory to gain research experience in the new field, the medical applications of radioisotopes. A radioisotope is the radioactive form of a chemical element. In 1942 Enrico Fermi had devised the first nuclear reactor, making it possible to generate large amounts of radioisotopes cheaply. By mid-1946, with the war over, radioisotopes became commercially available, and the field of nuclear medicine took off.

It was through Dr. Quimby that Rosalyn Yalow met Dr. G. Failla, dean of American medical physicists. After talking for a while with Dr. Yalow, Dr. Failla telephoned Dr. Bernard Roswit, chief of the Radiotherapy Service at the Bronx Veterans Administration Hospital, and said to him, "Bernie, if you want to set up a radioisotope service, I have someone here you must hire." In this way Rosalyn Yalow joined the Bronx VA as a part-time consultant in December 1947; she kept her position at Hunter College until the spring of 1950. During those years, while she was teaching full time at Hunter, she equipped and developed the radioisotope service at the VA hospital and started research projects together with Dr. Roswit and other physicians in the hospital. As a result of their work, the VA set up radioisotope services in several of its hospitals around the country.

In January 1950 Rosalyn Yalow left teaching and joined the Bronx VA full time. That spring Dr. Solomon A. Berson, who was completing his residency in internal medicine at the Bronx VA hospital, met Dr. Yalow and became very interested in what she was doing. That July he joined her in the radioisotope service of the hospital and thus began a twenty-two-year partnership that lasted until his death on April 11, 1972. Unfortunately he did

*Dr. Rosalyn S. Yalow*

133

*Dr. Rosalyn S. Yalow*

not survive to share the Nobel Prize with Dr. Rosalyn Yalow as he would have had he lived. The Nobel Prize is awarded only to living persons.

After Dr. Berson joined the service, Rosalyn Yalow gave up her work with the others and concentrated on their joint researches. Their first investigation was the application of radioisotopes in the determination of blood volume in the body and the clinical diagnosis of thyroid diseases as it was affected by iodine metabolism. After a while it seemed obvious to apply these methods to smaller peptides—i.e., the hormones. Insulin was the hormone most readily available in a highly purified form. Through their experiments they soon found that diabetic patients who were being injected with animal insulin were developing antibodies to the animal insulin. An antibody is a substance developed by the body to protect it against a foreign substance. In this case the foreign substance was the animal insulin. The antibodies were interfering with the body's making use of the animal insulin.

In studying the reaction of insulin with antibodies, Drs. Berson and Yalow felt that they had developed a tool that was capable of measuring the amount of insulin in the blood. Up to that point substances such as hormones, present in the blood and body tissues, could not be measured by methods then available because they were present in such infinitesimal amounts. As one scientist put it, it was like trying to detect the presence of half a lump of sugar in a lake about sixty-two miles long and wide and thirty feet deep! It took Drs. Berson and Yalow several more years to transform the idea of measuring insulin in the human body into a reality. Thus, the era of

*Dr. Rosalyn S. Yalow*

radioimmunoassay, as they called their new method, can be said to have begun in 1959.

In a simplified explanation, the measuring technique of radioimmunoassay (RIA) involves combining a natural hormone in the human body with its antibody, which results in a competition between the two substances. Then a small amount of the radioactive form of the hormone is introduced. By measuring how much of the radioactive form survives, and it can be measured with extreme accuracy, in competition with the antibody, researchers can tell how much of the natural hormone was present in the body to begin with.

Radioimmunoassay (RIA) is considered one of the most important advances in basic research which has been directly applied to clinical medicine. It is in use in more than 4,000 laboratories in this country alone, and also in thousands abroad, for identifying and measuring the concentration of hundreds of substances that could not be measured before. RIA is an application of nuclear physics in medicine. The method measures substances at concentrations as low as one-thousand-billionth of a gram (there are approximately 454 grams in 1 pound). Because of this new method, doctors are helped to diagnose conditions in their patients that previously escaped detection because the known methods were too crude to measure the seemingly trivial changes in the amount of hormones that can so drastically affect an individual's health.

The use of this test is continuing to lead to new discoveries and understandings of the nature of people. It is used by thousands of blood banks to detect and remove blood that is contaminated with the hepatitis virus from use in transfusions. Before this, many patients were infected with hepatitis after they received a transfusion of blood contaminated with the hepatitis virus.

As has been said, blood and body tissues contain many chemical substances—such as hormones, vitamins, and enzymes—which are vital to the proper functioning of the body but the concentration of which is too low to be measured without radioimmunoassay. Therefore, the role of these substances in health and disease could not previously be clearly understood. By measuring the differences between what is normal in health and what is abnormal in disease, RIA can determine what changes have taken place between the normal and the disease states. It can thus contribute to the clinical diagnosis of a disease.

When the amount of insulin in the blood was measured by the RIA method, some unexpected results were obtained. The adult type of diabetic was found to have a higher than usual level of insulin in the blood. Until that time it was believed that adult diabetics had a deficiency of insulin in their blood. RIA revealed that the increase in blood sugar in adult diabetics is due to some still unknown factor that interferes with the action of insulin and not to an insulin deficiency.

Other applications of the RIA method in studies on the role of hormones include the determination of whether the small size of certain children is due to their having too small an amount of a hormone concerned with growth, and whether their growth rate could be increased by treatment with growth hormone; the determination of whether too much secretion by the adrenal gland is due to a tumor of the gland or to an overactive pituitary gland; and the determination of whether sterility is due to the

*Dr. Rosalyn S. Yalow*

lack of production of a sufficient amount of sex hormones in the body.

RIA has been used to measure the degree of protection which an antirabies injection affords the victim of a bite. It has been used to determine if drugs are present in the blood in the case of a suspected drug addict. RIA has even had a dramatic place in criminology. Part of the evidence against Dr. "X," Mario Jascalevich, accused of murdering his patients with curare (who was later acquitted), came from an RIA that showed traces of the drug in the tissues from the victims' exhumed bodies.

With the technique of RIA, physicians and investigators in all areas of biological science were given a tool which has brought about an explosion of new information leading to fresh insight and understanding in almost every aspect of medicine. Rosalyn Yalow's husband, Aaron, a physics professor at Cooper Union and a radiation physicist at New York's Hospital for Joint Diseases, proudly describes his wife's work as "one of the most important discoveries of the century."

In answer to a reporter's question, Dr. Rosalyn Yalow said, "We did not patent the RIA method. Scientists don't always think of things as being patentable. We made a scientific discovery. Once it was published, it was open to the world."

Dr. Berson left the radioisotope service laboratory at the VA in 1968 to take on the chairmanship of the department of medicine at the Mount Sinai School of Medicine. Recently Dr. Rosalyn Yalow said that she had had no idea where her and Dr. Berson's research would lead when, in 1950, they began their twenty-two-year collaboration. "It was a great partnership—he wanted to be a physicist, and I wanted to be a physician." In April 1972 Dr. Solomon

Berson died of a heart attack in his hotel room at a medical meeting in Atlantic City, New Jersey, at the age of fifty-three.

Rosalyn Yalow continued to do research and to publish. Between 1972 and 1976 she won a dozen medical awards in her own right, and in 1976 she became the first woman to win the Albert Lasker Basic Medical Research Award.

It was 6:45 in the morning of October 13, 1977, and Dr. Yalow was already at work at her desk at the Bronx VA hospital, in the middle of one of her "normal seventy-hour weeks," when the telephone call came from Stockholm to tell her that she had been awarded the Nobel Prize in medicine. In December of that year she and her husband traveled to Stockholm to receive the award. There was a blare of trumpets as she rose to receive the gold medal and diploma and to shake hands with King Carl XVI Gustaf.

While Dr. Yalow was in Stockholm, she was asked to address the students there. She took the opportunity to speak about discrimination against women. She said, in part, "Among students, women are represented in reasonable proportion to their numbers in the community; yet among the scientists, scholars and leaders of our world they are not. No objective testing has revealed such substantial differences in talent as to account for this discrepancy. . . . The failure of women to have reached positions of leadership has been due in large part to social and professional discrimination. In the past, few women have tried and even fewer have succeeded. We still live in a world in which a significant fraction of people, including women, believe that a woman belongs and wants to belong exclusively in the home." Again, in the same

*Dr. Rosalyn S. Yalow*

139

address, she said, "The world cannot afford the loss of the talents of half its people if we are to solve the many problems which beset us. We bequeath to you, the next generation, our knowledge but also our problems. While we still live, let us join hands, hearts, and minds to work together for their solution so that your world will be better than ours and the world of your children even better."

The Bronx VA Hospital is now affiliated with the Mount Sinai School of Medicine, where Dr. Rosalyn Yalow holds the title of Distinguished Service Professor and where she is still very active. It is certain that she will be heard from again in the scientific future.

sixty men aboard the research vessel *Anton Bruun*, she now became the *first* and *only* woman to become a mission leader in the Tektite II project. The Greek word *tektos* means "molten." Tektites are defined as any of several kinds of small glassy bodies, in various forms, the exact origin of which is not known. They are believed to come from meteorites and are found on land and on ocean floors. The aim of the Tektite project was to increase knowledge of the sea and to investigate means of exploring outer space by studying the behavior of crews living and working in isolated and confined quarters. Because of its application to journey in outer space, the National Aeronautics and Space Administration was among the government agencies that collaborated on the project with various universities. The overall direction was under the United States Department of the Interior.

Tektite I had taken place in 1969, when four scientists spent two months in an underwater habitat, testing equipment and demonstrating that humans had the technical capacity to explore below the surface of the seas for long periods of time. There were seventeen Tektite II teams, and one of them was a five-women team led by Dr. Sylvia Mead. The other sixteen were male-only teams.

When Dr. Mead joined the Tektite II project, she had about seventeen years of diving experience—more than 1,000 hours of scuba and Hooka-style apparatus diving. This record was neither surpassed nor even equaled by any others on the project—men or women. Dr. Mead's team of female aquanauts lived underwater for two weeks near St. John, Virgin Islands, on the floor of Great Lameshur Bay. The other members of Dr. Mead's team were Dr. Renate Schlenz True, age thirty-three, who holds a doctorate in oceanography; Ann Hurley Hartline, age

*Dr. Sylvia Earle Mead*

twenty-three, a graduate student in marine ecology at the Scripps Institution of Oceanography, University of California, at San Diego; Alina Szmant, age twenty-four, who holds a master's degree in marine biology from Scripps; and Margaret Ann Lucas, age twenty-three, an electrical engineer then studying for a master's degree in ocean engineering at the University of Delaware.

From July 6 to 20, 1970, the women lived in a stark white habitat, built by the General Electric Company, which resembled two large cylindrical storage tanks. The two structures were joined together by a tunnel. "It was the safest two weeks of my life," said Dr. Mead. "We went as scientists primarily and as women secondarily, but the only thing men could do down there that we couldn't do was grow beards." Aside from a very minor earthquake, it was not too different from living on terra firma. Most of them lost a few pounds. The one smoker among them had to give up her habit because her cigarette would not stay lighted—not enough oxygen.

Although the actual descent below water did not take place until July 6, Dr. Mead arrived at the Tektite base camp early in June to help plan the two-week predive training period. A sixty-five-pound rebreather apparatus, which recycled the air continuously, had just been designed by General Electric. Oxygen was added as needed, and carbon dioxide was eliminated as it formed. Besides permitting the diver to stay under water for a longer period of time, the rebreather did not give off bubbles to scare off the fish as did the scuba tank. It was a tremendous improvement. Speaking of the training period, Dr. Mead said, "Although a particular effort was made to treat male and female aquanauts alike, it soon became clear that we were receiving an unusual amount of protective interest, well-intended but sometimes harassing. Mostly we joked about it."

On July 6, at a signal from Dr. Mead, the five women aquanauts made their descent to the habitat anchored to the floor of Great Lameshur Bay fifty feet below its surface. All the time during their two-week stay under water, closed-circuit monitoring television cameras, manned by NASA scientists, studied the behavior of the crews working under the stress of rigid isolation. The work load of the women was no lighter than that of the male teams. They were in constant communication with the monitoring scientists on the shore and were required to clear work plans before every dive.

From six to ten hours each day were spent outside the habitat. Each dive itself was confined to four hours, during which time they could go out to a range of 1,500 feet from the habitat to observe marine plant and animal life. They always went in teams of two—the buddy system—for safety. With the presence of a full moon at the time, the view from below the clear water was breathtaking.

In her report to the Department of the Interior, Dr. Mead stated, "Thirty-five species of plant-eating fishes in fourteen families were observed in Lameshur Bay during Tektite II Mission. One hundred and fifty-four species of marine plants were found, including twenty-six species newly reported for the Virgin Islands. Activities of the fishes were noted, particularly feeding behavior and choice of diet, and their influence on vegetation assessed. Fish distribution was described and compared with plant distribution. In general, attached vegetation was abun-

*Dr. Sylvia Earle Mead*

dant where herbivores [animals, like fish, that feed on plants] were sparse, and where herbivores were abundant, vegetation was sparse."

In another part of her report, Dr. Mead pointed out that much was learned from the Tektite II program about working under water. "Under normal circumstances a person can spend less than an hour at a depth of one hundred feet in the course of a day; less than two hours at fifty feet, but, working from an underwater base, tissues saturated with the compressed air breathed, a diver has virtually unlimited diving time at depth. This makes it possible for the first time to work under water in a manner comparable in time to working conditions on land. It is possible, therefore, to accomplish in two weeks' diving time what would take two months or more if using scuba from the surface, even under the most favorable surface conditions."

Dr. Mead finished her report with these words, "Much has been learned about the marine environment by working from ships, from shore-based laboratories. More insight came with the development of scuba and various submersibles that actually put men into the water. I regard underwater habitats as the logical next step, the reasonable approach to exploring and coming to understand the aquatic environment. The technique has come none too soon."

On July 20, after two weeks under water, Dr. Mead's team of women came up to the surface and spent twenty hours in a decompression chamber. When they finally emerged, they were "wined and dined" unlike their male counterparts. Newspapers, radio, and television all over the country sang their praises. It was what Dr. Mead

*Dr. Sylvia Earle Mead*

termed an example of "reverse discrimination." There were ceremonies and receptions around the country, accompanied by press conferences. The women made television appearances, gave talks before Congress, and were even invited to lunch in the White House. They were presented with the Conservation Service Award, the highest honor of the United States Department of the Interior, by Secretary of the Interior Walter J. Hickel.

When asked about meeting sharks under water, Dr. Mead said that they often met sharks in their underwater studies but that she never had any trouble with them. Perhaps the movie *Jaws* has given some false ideas about sharks.

Asked about prejudice against women in her field of marine biology, Dr. Mead believes that women already have the opportunity to advance in their professions if they are willing to work hard, as she does. "I do think a woman has to have a little thicker skin in trying to get into some fields," she maintains, "but once you reach a certain point of achievement, the stares and jokes stop, and you are recognized for the merits of your contributions." She sees no reason why mixed teams of men and women, chosen for "competence and compatibility of interests," should not be used on future projects like Tektite.

Dr. Mead's interests and activities are many and varied. In 1971, after Tektite, she was consultant to the Smithsonian Tropical Research Institute for the study of the ecology of the marine plants of Panama. The year 1972 was also busy. During it she was chief scientist on the research vessel *Searcher* on an expedition to the Galápagos and Cocos islands for the study and collection of marine plants (January and February); chief scientist and aquanaut of the Flare Project in the Florida Keys for research on reef plants (March and April); consultant to the Scientist-in-the-Sea Program in Panama City, Florida, where she participated as instructor in scientific diving techniques (August); and participant in the National Academy of Sciences workshop in manned undersea science and technology (October). In the midst of it all, she found time to lecture at the University of California at Los Angeles on "Diving Marine Mammals" and "The Biology of Catalina Island."

In June 1973 Dr. Mead went on a study-observation visit to the People's Republic of China, where she represented the American Women for International Understanding. She traveled as one of fourteen professional women to six cities in eastern China to establish contact with professional colleagues. Upon her return she lectured at UCLA on "Science in the People's Republic of China."

Keeping to an increasingly busy schedule, Dr. Mead served as chief scientist and aquanaut for three diving projects using the underwater laboratory Hydrolab in Freeport, Bahamas, to study marine life. These projects took place in February 1973, July 1974, and August 1974. Again, in April 1975, she was chief scientist and aquanaut of the Score Project, again using Hydrolab to study marine plants and animals.

From 1970 to 1976 Dr. Mead gave more than 200 lectures on marine ecology and technology at universities, institutions, elementary and secondary schools, and civic and professional organizations in various parts of the United States and Canada. She participated in about fifty television programs. Other activities during 1975 included participation in the California Academy of

*Dr. Sylvia Earle Mead*

Sciences Coelacanth Expedition to the Comoro Islands (February and March); participation in the Smithsonian Institution's IMSWE project at Carrie Bow Cay (May); and conducting the National Geographic–Sea Films research project on sunken ships as artificial reefs in Truk Lagoon, Eastern Caroline Islands (June and July).

Because of her expertise and vast background of experience in marine biology, Dr. Mead was invited to speak at important international conferences such as the fourteenth International Underwater Symposium in Stockholm, Sweden; the Ocean's 1976 Conference in Melbourne, Australia; the World Wildlife Fund, Fourth International Congress in San Francisco; and the Ocean's 1977 Conference in Melbourne. She was the subject of a number of educational films, including *The Aquamaids of Tektite II, The Sea People, Women in the World of Work,* and *People with Purpose.* A summary of this busy scientist's diving experience includes more than 1,000 hours using compressed air and oxygen and nitrogen mixtures, more than 2,500 hours using hooka, helmets, and scuba, and more than 50 hours using the General Electric rebreather.

Giles Mead was formerly curator of fish at the Harvard Museum of Comparative Zoology and has a doctorate in zoology from Stanford University. He is a high-seas oceanographer and a specialist in deep-sea fish. While it is not often that Dr. Mead and her husband (who is at present the director of the Los Angeles County Museum of Natural History, where she is an associate in botany) work on the same project, they did get together on the Smithsonian's Man-in-Sea Project, and both went diving in the Bahamas from a submarine, the *Deep River.* She was the only woman aboard.

Dr. Sylvia Mead's principal research interests are the interrelationships between marine plants and animals. Marine mammal behavior and the ecology and evolution of deepwater marine plants are also subjects of her research. She is very interested in the problem of ocean pollution and is convinced that the exploration of the seas is crucial to human survival.

At present she is carrying on research in several areas: the seasonal aspects of deepwater kelp forests at Catalina Island (in collaboration with James Coyer, Alexandra Zangg, and Alfred Giddings); the distribution and ecology of the marine algae of the Galápagos Islands (in collaboration with Paul Silva of the University of California at Berkeley); the distribution, ecology, and systematics of marine algae of the Juan Fernández and San Félix Islands in Chile (in collaboration with Joy Morrill of the Philadelphia Academy of Natural Sciences); the ecology and distribution of plants and herbivores along vertical escarpments of the Bahamas, based on Hydrolab observations; the ecology, distribution, and systematics of marine plants occurring in the Florida Middlegrounds in the Gulf of Mexico (in collaboration with Tom Hopkins of the University of Alabama and Susan Brawley of the University of California at Berkeley); the documentation of the marine plants of the Comoro Islands (in collaboration with field studies by John McCosker of the California Academy of Sciences); and the documentation of the songs and behavior of humpback whales (in collaboration with Roger Payne, Katherine Payne, Peter Tyack, and Alfred Giddings).

Asked whether she considers herself feminine, Dr. Mead says, "What is 'feminine'? I enjoy being a woman. I love my children and my husband and am happy as

*Dr. Sylvia Earle Mead*

153

mother and wife. If this is feminine, I am feminine. If one must appear empty-headed and assume helpless dependence to be feminine, then I am not."

At home, Dr. Mead works best between eleven o'clock in the evening and three o'clock in the morning, when the family is asleep. She has often got by on two or three hours of sleep for several days in a row when she is on a project.

Many honors and awards have come to Dr. Mead. In addition to the Conservation Service Award from the United States Department of the Interior (1970), she received the County of Los Angeles Commendation (1970), was named Woman of the Year by the Los Angeles Times (1970), received the Meritorious Service Award from the Natural History Museum of Los Angeles County (1970), the Angel of Distinction Award from the Central City Association of Los Angeles, the Boston Sea Rovers Award (1972), a Certificate of Tribute from the Los Angeles County Board of Supervisors (1975), the NOGI award in science from the Underwater Society of America (1976), and the Oceanus Award (1977). In 1976 she was named a Fellow of the California Academy of Sciences.

As much as Dr. Mead has already contributed and is presently contributing to the science of marine biology, it is the feeling of the author that much more will be heard from her in the future. As she has said, "There is an enormous amount to be learned about the sea; like most wilderness, it has great potential."

# Professional Women's Groups

Academy of Management
> Committee on the Status of Women in the Management Profession
> 2700 Bay Area Boulevard, Houston, Texas 77058

Adult Education Association of the U.S.
> Commission on the Status of Women in Adult Education
> 810 18th Street, NW, Washington D.C. 20006

American Alliance for Health, Physical Education and Recreation
> Task Force on Equal Opportunity & Human Rights
> 1201 16th Street, NW, Washington, D.C. 20036

American Anthropological Association
> Committee on the Status of Women in Anthropology
> 1703 New Hampshire Avenue, N.W., Washington, D.C. 20009

American Association for the Advancement of Science
> Office of Opportunities in Science
> 1776 Massachusetts Avenue, NW, Washington, D.C. 20036

American Association of Immunologists
> Women and Minority Immunologists
> 9650 Rockville Pike, Bethesda, Md. 20014

American Association of University Women
    2401 Virginia Avenue, NW, Washington, D.C. 20037
American Chemical Society
    Women Chemists Committee
    1155 16th Street, NW, Washington, D.C. 20036
American Federation of Teachers
    Women's Rights Committee
    11 Dupont Circle, NW, Washington, D.C. 20036
American Geological Institute
    Women Geoscientists Committee
    5205 Leesburg Pike, Falls Church, Va. 22041
American Institute of Architects
    Women in Architecture Task Force
    1735 New York Avenue, NW, Washington, D.C. 20006
American Institute of Chemists
    Professional Opportunities for Women Committee
    7315 Wisconsin Avenue, Bethesda, Md. 20014
American Medical Women's Association, Inc.
    1740 Broadway, New York, N.Y. 10019
American Nurse's Association
    2420 Pershing Drive, Kansas City, Mo. 64105
American Physical Society
    Committee on Women in Physics
    Lab of Physics, Harvard University, Cambridge, Mass.
    02138
American Physiological Society
    Task Force on Women in Physiology
    9650 Rockville Pike, Bethesda, Md. 20014
American Psychiatric Association
    Committee on Women
    1700 18th Street, NW, Washington, D.C. 20009
American Psychological Association
    Committee on Women in Psychology
    1200 17th Street, NW, Washington, D.C. 20036

*Professional Women's Groups*

American Public Health Association, Inc.
Women's Caucus
1015 18th Street, NW, Washington, D.C. 20036
American Society for Cell Biology
Women in Cell Biology
Department of Biology, Yale University, New Haven,
Conn. 06520
American Society for Microbiology
Committee on Status of Women Microbiologists
1913 I Street, NW, Washington, D.C. 20006
American Society of Biological Chemists
Committee on Status of Women
9650 Rockville Pike, Bethesda, Md. 20014
Association for Women in Mathematics
Mills College, Oakland, Calif. 94613
Association for Women in Psychology
Manhattan Community College, 180 West End Avenue,
New York, N.Y. 10023
Association for Women in Science
1346 Connecticut Avenue, NW, Washington, D.C. 20036
Association of American Women Dentists
435 North Michigan Avenue, Chicago, Ill. 60611
Association of Women in Architecture
P.O. Box 1, Dayton, Mo. 63105
Biophysical Society
Committee on Professional Opportunities for Women
George Washington University Medical School, Washing-
ton, D.C. 20037
National Dental Association
Ladies' Auxiliary
P.O. Box 197, Charlottesville, Va. 22902
National Education Association
Women's Caucus
1201 16th Street, NW, Washington, D.C. 20036

*Professional Women's Groups*

Society of Women Engineers
  United Engineering Center
  345 East 47th Street, New York, N.Y. 10017
Women Architects, Landscape Architects, and Planners
  Boston Architecture Center, 320 Newbury Street, Boston,
    Mass. 02115
Women in Science and Engineering
  22 Turning Mill Road, Lexington, Mass. 02173

*Professional Women's Groups*

# Bibliography

Bernard, Jessie. *Academic Women*. Pennsylvania State University Press, 1964.

Bluemel, Elinor. *Florence Sabin: Colorado Woman of the Century*. University of Colorado Press, 1959.

Borer, Mary I. *Women Who Made History*. F. Warne, 1963.

Born, Max. "Recollections of Max Born." *Bulletin of the Atomic Scientists* (September, October, November 1965).

Boynick, David K. *Pioneers in Petticoats*. Crowell, 1959.

———. *Women Who Led the Way*. Crowell, 1972.

Brown, Hazen. *Transactions New York Academy of Sciences*, ser. II, vol. 19, no. 5 (March 1957), pp. 447–56.

Brunton, Lauder. "Some Women in Medicine." *Canadian Medical Association Journal*, vol. XLVIII (1943), pp. 60–65.

Burgess, Mary W. *Contribution of Women*. Dillon Press, 1975.

Chandler, Caroline. *Famous Men of Medicine*. Dodd, 1950.

Chenoweth, Alice D. "Women in Medicine." *Journal of American Medical Women's Association*, vol. XXIII, no. 12 (1968).

Corn, J. K. "Alice Hamilton, M.D., and Women's Welfare." *New England Journal of Medicine* (February 5, 1976) pp. 316–18.

Crawford, Deborah. *Lise Meitner, Atomic Pioneer*. Crown, 1969.

Dash, Joan. *A Life of One's Own.* Harper & Row, 1973.

Davis, Audrey. *Bibliography on Women with Special Emphasis on Their Roles in Science & Society.* Science History Publications, 1974.

Douglas, Emily T. *Remember the Ladies.* Putnam, 1966.

Edwards, Ralph W. "The First Woman Dentist: Lucy Hobbs Taylor, D.D.S.—1883–1910." *Bulletin of History of Medicine,* vol. 25 (1951).

Elia, Joseph J. "Alice Hamilton 1869–1970." *New England Journal of Medicine,* vol. 283 (1970), pp. 993–994.

Emerson, Gladys A. "The Effect of Vitamin E Deficiency upon Growth." *Journal of Nutrition,* vol. 14 (1937), p. 169.

Evans, H. M., and O. H. Emerson and G. A. Emerson. "The Isolation from Wheat Germ Oil of an Alcohol, Alphatocopherol, Having the Properties of Vitamin E." *Journal of Biological Chemistry,* vol. 113 (1936), p. 319.

Fermi, Laura. *Atoms in the Family.* University of Chicago Press, 1954.

————. *Illustrious Immigrants: The Intellectual Migration from Europe, 1930–1941.* University of Chicago Press, 1968.

Fleming, Alice. *Doctors in Petticoats.* Lippincott, 1964.

Fleming, Donald, and B. Bailyn. *The Intellectual Migration: Europe and America, 1930–1960.* Harvard University Press, 1969.

Forsee, Aylesa. *Women Who Reached for Tomorrow.* Macrae Smith, 1960.

Frithiof, Patricia. *Women in Science.* University of Lund, 1967.

Grant, Madeleine P. *Alice Hamilton, Pioneer Doctor in Industrial Medicine.* Abelard-Schuman, 1968.

Haber, Julia M. *Women in the Biological Sciences.* University of Pennsylvania Press, 1939.

Haber, Louis. *Black Pioneers of Science and Invention.* Harcourt Brace Jovanovich, 1970.

Hahn, Otto. *My Life, the Autobiography of a Scientist.* Herder and Herder, 1970.

Hall, Mary H. "An American Mother and the Nobel Prize."

*Bibliography*

*McCall's* (July 1964).

Hamilton, Alice. *Industrial Toxicology*, 3rd ed. P.S.G. Publishing Co., 1970.

———. "Pioneering in Industrial Medicine." *Journal of the American Medical Women's Association*, vol. 2 (1947).

———. and Charles Verrill. *Hygiene of the Printing Trades.* Government Printing Office, 1917.

———. *Exploring the Dangerous Trades: The Autobiography of Alice Hamilton, M.D.* Little Brown & Company, 1943.

———. "A Woman of Ninety Looks at Her World." *The Atlantic* (March 1965).

———. "Because War Breeds War," in *Why Wars Must Cease.* Macmillan, 1935.

———. "Edith and Alice Hamilton—Students in Germany." *Atlantic Monthly*, vol. 215 (March 1965), pp. 124–32.

———. *Women in the Lead Industries.* Government Printing Office, February 1919.

Hayden, Robert C., and Jacqueline Harris. *Nine Black American Doctors.* Addison-Wesley Publishing Company, 1976.

Hazen, Elizabeth L., and Rachel Brown. "Two Antifungal Agents Produced by a Soil Actinomycete." *Science*, vol. 112 (1950), p. 423.

Hollingworth, Harry. *Leta Stetter Hollingworth: A Biography.* University of Nebraska Press, 1943.

Hollingworth, Leta S. *The Psychology of Subnormal Children.* Macmillan Company, 1920.

———. *The Psychology of the Adolescent.* D. Appleton, 1928.

———. *Gifted Children.* Macmillan Company, 1926.

———. *Gifted Children.* Macmillan Company, 1926.

———. *Children Above 180 I.Q.*, completed by her husband. World Book Company, 1942.

———. "Contributions to Education," no. 69, Bureau of Publications, Teachers College, Columbia University, 1914.

Hume, Ruth F. *Great Women of Medicine.* Random House, 1964.

Hunt, Caroline. *Ellen Richards.* Whitcomb & Barrows, 1912.

*Bibliography*

Ireland, Norma O. *Index to Women of the World.* F. W. Faxon Company, 1970.

Jeffery, G. A. "Nobel Prize in Chemistry Awarded to Crystallographer." *Science,* vol. 146 (November 6, 1964), pp. 748–749.

Kendall, Phebe M. *Maria Mitchell, Life, Letters and Journals.* Boston, 1896.

Kinsler, Miriam S. "The American Woman Dentist: A Brief Historical Review From 1855 to 1968." *Bulletin of History of Dentistry,* vol. 17 (December 1969).

Kundsin, Ruth, ed. *Women and Success.* William Morrow & Company, 1974.

Larsen, Egon. *Inventor's Scrapbook.* Drummond, 1947.

Lerner, Gerda. *Bibliography in the History of American Women,* 2nd ed. Sarah Lawrence College, 1975.

Logan, Myra. "Aureomycin in Soft Tissue Infections." *American Journal of Surgery* (February 1950).

———. "Intestinal Obstruction in Infancy and Childhood." *Harlem Hospital Bulletin* (1952).

Lopate, Carol. *Women in Medicine.* Johns Hopkins Press, 1968.

Lovejoy, Esther Pohl. *Women Doctors of the World.* Macmillan Company, 1957.

Mattfeld, Jacquelyn, and Carol Van Aken. *Women and the Scientific Professions.* MIT Press, 1965.

Mattfield, Jacquelyn, ed. *MIT Symposium on American Women in Science.* MIT Press, 1964.

Marks, Geoffrey. *Women in White.* Charles Scribner's Sons, 1972.

Mayer, Maria G. "The Structure of the Nucleus." *Scientific American* (March 1951).

Meitner, Lise. "Looking Back." *Bulletin of Atomic Scientists* (November 1964), pp. 2–7.

——— and O. R. Frisch. "Disintegration of Uranium by Neutrons: A New Type of Nuclear Reaction." *Nature,* vol. 143 (1939), p. 239.

*Bibliography*

Mozans, H. J. *Women in Science*. MIT Press, 1974.

Osen, Lynn. *Women in Mathematics*. MIT Press, 1974.

Phelan, M. K. *Probing the Unknown: The Story of Dr. Florence Sabin*. Crowell, 1969.

Renshaw, Josephine E., and Maryland Pennell. "Distribution of Women Physicians, 1969." *The Woman Physician*, vol. XXVI, no. 4 (1971).

Rickey, Elinor. *Eminent Women of the West*. Howell-North, 1975.

Riedman, Sarah. *Men and Women Behind the Atom*. Abelard-Schuman, 1958.

Rossiter, Margaret. "Women Scientists in America Before 1920." *American Scientist*, vol. 62, no. 1 (May–June 1974).

Russell, M. P. "James Barry 1792–1865, Inspector General of Army Hospitals." *Edinburgh Medical Journal*, vol. 50 (1943).

Schwartz, Walter. "The Amazing Mrs. Hodgkin." *The Observer* (December 13, 1964), pp. 11–16.

Shippen, Katherine B. *Bright Design*. Viking, 1949, pp. 126–28.

Shryock, Richard H. "Women in American Medicine." *Journal of the American Medical Women's Association*, vol. V (1950), pp. 371–79.

Stoddard, Hope. *Famous American Women*. Crowell, 1970.

Stone, Elizabeth. "A Mme. Curie from the Bronx." *New York Times Magazine* (April 9, 1978), pp. 29–36.

Talbott, John H. *Biographical History of Medicine*. Grune and Stratton, 1970.

Teitz, Joyce. *What's a Nice Girl Like You Doing in a Place Like This!* Coward-McCann, 1972, pp. 100–23.

United States National Science Foundation. *Women in Scientific Careers*. Government Printing Office, 1961.

Willard, Mary L. *Pioneer Women in Chemistry*. University of Pennsylvania Press, 1940.

Wigner, Eugene P. "Maria Goeppert Mayer." *Physics Today* (May 1972).

*Bibliography*

Wilson, Dorothy. *Palace of Healing: The Story of Dr. Clara Swain, First Woman Missionary Doctor.* McGraw-Hill, 1968.

Wilson, Mitchell. "How Nobel Prize Winners Get That Way." *Atlantic Monthly* (December 1969), pp. 69–74.

Wright, Jane C. "A Visit to Kenya and Tanganyika in 1961." *Journal of the National Medical Association*, vol. 53, no. 4 (July 1961), pp. 327–34.

——. "Women in Medicine." A speech.

——. "Clinical Drug Dosages and Duration of Therapy of the Cancer Chemotherapeutic Agents." *Cancer Chemotherapy Reports*, no. 16 (February 1962).

——. "The Current Status of Chemotherapy and Hormone Therapy for Cancer," *Progress in Clinical Cancer.* Grune & Stratton, Inc., 1965.

——. "Dr. Jane C. Wright Returns to New York Medical College as Associate Dean." *Intercom, New York Medical College*, vol. 1, no. 4 (1967).

Wupperman, Alice. "Woman in 'American Men of Science.' " *Journal of Chemical Education*, vol. 18 (1941), pp. 120–121.

Yost, Edna. *Women of Modern Science.* Dodd, Mead, 1959.

### General References

*American Men of Science*

*American Men and Women in Science*

*Biography Index*

*Current Biography*

*Dictionary of Scientific Biography*, C. C. Gillespie, ed., 1974

*A Biographical Dictionary of Scientists*, T. I. Williams, ed., 1974

*Encyclopedia of World Biography*

*Encyclopedia of Science and Technology*

*Negro Handbook*

*Notable American Women 1607–1950*, E. T. James, ed., 1971

*Bibliography*

*Project on the Status and Education of Women*, Association of
American Colleges, 1818 R Street, N.W., Washington, D.C.
20009

*National Cyclopedia of American Biography Current*

*Reference Biography Service*, British Information Services,
London

*Survey and Evaluation of Registries of Women in the Professions*, Federation of Organizations for Professional
Women, 1346 Connecticut Avenue, N.W., Washington,
D.C. 20036, Room 1122

*Who's Who in America*

*Who's Who in the World*

*Who's Who of American Women*

*Who's Who in the East*

*World Who's Who of Women*

*World Who's Who in Science*

## Women's Periodicals

*Atlantis*, a women's studies journal

*Collegiate Woman's Career Magazine*

*Feminist Bulletin*

*Feminist Press*

*Feminist Studies*

*Prime-time*, an independent feminist monthly

*Quest*, a feminist quarterly

*U.S. Women's Bureau Bulletins*, 1918 to date (government
publications)

U.S. Bureau of the Census, *A Statistical Portrait of Women in
the U.S.*, Washington, 1976

*Women's Agenda*

*Women's Studies*, an interdisciplinary journal

*Women's Studies Newsletter*

*Women's Work*

*Bibliography*

# Index

Addams, Jane, 14
Alpha particle, 43
Alston, Charles, 102, 104
American College of Surgeons, 97
Argonne National Laboratory, 93
Arthur R. Logan Memorial Hospital, 98
Aspasia, 3
Atom, structure of, 43
Atomic bomb, 49–50, 92–93

Barringer, Emily Dunning, 7
Barry, James, 4
Becquerel, Antoine Henri, 44
Bernal, J. D., 107
Berson, Dr. Solomon A., 133, 138–139
Beta particle, 43
Bird, Patricia, 144
Blackwell, Elizabeth, 6, 8
Bohr, Niels, 47, 49, 85, 89, 94
Born, Max, 84, 88
Bragg, Sir William and Sir Lawrence, 110
Bronx Veterans Hospital, 133
Brookhaven National Laboratory, 131
Brown-Hazen Fund, 68
Brown, Rachel Fuller
    awards and honors, 71

chemist in New York State
    Department of Health, 64
childhood, 63
commitment to science, 63
and discovery of nystatin, 67
and Dr. Elizabeth Hazen, 66
doctoral degree, 64
nystatin and Dutch elm disease, 70
nystatin and restoration of art
    treasures, 70
and Research Corporation, 67, 68
Streptomyces noursei, 67
Burt, Sir Cyril, xvi

Carson, Rachel, 9
Chadwick, James, 44
Chain, Dr. Ernst B., 109, 110
Chemotherapy, 119
Chinn, Dr. May E., 10
Conant, James, 92
Cori, Carl and Gerty, xiv
Crick, F. H., xv
Curie, Eve, 129
Curie, Marie and Pierre, xiii, xv, 3, 44, 129

Dalldorf Fellowship, 68
Domagk, Gerhard, 109
Dorfman, Professor D. D., xvi

Einstein, Albert, 88, 89
Elizabeth Hazen Scholarship, 68
Emerson, Gladys Anderson
  chairman of department of home
    economics at UCLA, 80
  and Dr. Herbert M. Evans, 77
  doctorate degree from University of
    California, Berkeley, 76
  early childhood, 73, 74
  fellowship in nutrition and
    biochemistry at University of
    California, Berkeley, 76
  head of animal nutrition depart-
    ment, Merck and Company, 79
  honors and awards, 81
  motivation toward the sciences, 75
  post doctoral fellow at University
    of Göttingen, 76
  research associate at Sloan-
    Kettering Institute, 79
  victim of sex discrimination, 80, 81
  war work in nutrition, 79
  work on vitamin E, 77
Evans, Dr. Herbert M., 77

Failla, Dr. G., 133
Fermi, Enrico, 46, 49, 84, 86, 88, 89,
  92, 93, 129, 133
Fleming, Alexander, 109
Florey, Howard, 109
Franck, James, 84, 88, 92
Franklin, Rosalind, xiv–xv
Fungus and disease, 65

Gamma rays, 43
Garrett, Mary Elizabeth, 7, 31
Garrison, William Lloyd, 5
Goldhaber, Dr. Gertrude, 131
Goldhaber, Dr. Maurice, 131
Göttingen University, 84, 86
Greene, Catherine, 5

Hahn, Dr. Otto, 42, 44, 46, 47, 48, 129
Hamilton, Alice
  appointed to faculty of Harvard
    Medical School, 1919, 24

and artificial silk industry, 26–27
and "dangerous trades," 15–16
early childhood and education,
  12–13
efforts to eliminate lead poisoning,
  18–22
in Germany in 1895, 13
honors and awards, 28
interest in industrial medicine, 15
Jane Addams and Hull House, 14,
  15
medical degree in 1893, 13
and "phossy jaw" disease, 16
study of dangers to women in
  industry, 27
trip to Soviet Union, 24–25
typhoid fever epidemic, 14
work on nitric acid in explosives
  industry, 22–23
Hartline, Ann Hurley, 145
Hazen, Elizabeth, 66
Hiroshima, 49, 93
Hodgkin, Dorothy Crowfoot
  children, 115
  doctorate degree from Cambridge in
    1937, 107
  early childhood and family
    background, 105
  honors and awards, 115
  marriage to Thomas Hodgkin in
    1937, 107–108, 115
  Nobel Prize in 1964, 114
  research fellowship at Oxford and
    Cambridge, 107
  structure of insulin molecule, 114
  work on penicillin, 108–110, 112,
    113
  work on vitamin $B_{12}$, 108
  work with J. D. Bernal at Cambridge
    University, 107
  X-ray analysis of vitamin $B_{12}$, 113
  X-ray diffraction, 110, 112
Hollingworth, Leta Stetter, xvi
  clinical psychologist at Bellevue
    Hospital in New York, 54, 55
  death from cancer, 61

*Index*

director of research at Speyer School, 60
early childhood, 52, 53
education of the gifted child, 59
experiment on "inferiority" of women, 56–58
graduate study at Columbia University, 54
honorary degree from her alma mater, 61
marriage to Harry Hollingworth, 54
supporter of women's suffrage, 58
teacher of educational psychology at Teachers College, Columbia, 59
teaching in Nebraska, 53
Hull House, 14, 15

Industrial medicine, 12, 15
Ingegno, Dr. Alfred P., 8
Insulin, 114

Jensen, Dr. Hans D., 94, 95
Joliot-Curie, Irene, xiv
Joliot, Frederic, xiv
Jones, David D., 119

Kaiser Wilhelm Institute, 46
Kies, Mary, 5

Lee, Rebecca, 8
Logan, Arthur R., 98
Logan, Harold, 103
Logan, Louise, 103
Logan, Myra Adele
death in 1977, 104
early background, 97
first black woman elected Fellow of American College of Surgeons, 97, 100
first woman surgeon to operate on the heart, 97, 100
internship and residency, 99
marriage to Charles Alston, 102–103
medical degree, 99
pioneer in group medicine, 100
professional affiliations, 103

research on new antibiotics, 100
scholarship to medical school, 98
study in breast cancer, 102
Lucas, Margaret Ann, 146

Manhattan Project, 49, 90, 92
Mall, Dr. Franklin Paine, 32
Maltby, Margaret, 9
Mather, Sarah, 5
Mayer, Maria Goeppert, xiv
collaboration with Hans D. Jensen, 94
death, 95
doctoral degree, 87
family background, 83
and Harold Urey, 89
marriage to Joseph Mayer, 87
move to Columbia University, 89
move to Johns Hopkins University, 87
move to University of California at San Diego, 95
move to University of Chicago, 92, 93
Nobel Prize in physics, 83, 95
nuclear fission and the atom bomb, 89–90
shell model of atomic nucleus, 93, 94
"Statistical Mechanics," 88
student at Göttingen University, 84
teacher at Sarah Lawrence College, 90
theory of guantum mechanics, 87–88
war research at Columbia University, 90
Mead, Margaret, 11
Mead, Sylvia Earle
college and graduate work, 142–143
early childhood and schooling, 141–142
honors and awards, 154
learning to scuba dive, 143
marriage to Giles W. Mead, 144
present research activities, 153

*Index*

Mead, Sylvia Earle (*cont.*)
  principal research interests, 153
  professional and scientific diving,
    143
  resident director of Mote Marine
    Laboratory, 144
  and Tektite II project, 144–151
  visit to China in 1973, 151
Meitner, Lise
  attitude toward the atomic bomb,
    49, 50
  death, 51
  discovery of protactinium, 46
  elected member of the Swedish
    Academy of Science, 50
  family background, 41
  fled Nazi Germany, 47
  head of physics department at
    Kaiser Wilhelm Institute, 46
  interest in radioactivity, 42
  and Max Planck, 42
  and Niels Bohr, 47, 49
  and nuclear fission, 41, 49
  and Otto Hahn, 42, 44, 46, 47, 48
  received the Enrico Fermi Award,
    51
  study on transmutation of
    chemical elements, 46
  work at Nobel Institute for Physics,
    48
  in the United States, 50, 51
Mitchell, Maria, 9

Nagasaki, 50, 93
Neutron, 44
Nuclear fission, 41
Nuclear medicine, 133
Nystatin, 67, 70, 71

Oppenheimer, Robert, 86

Penicillin, 108–110, 112
Planck, Max, 42
Price, Leontyne, 103, 104
Proton, 44

Quimby, Dr. Edith, 132

Rachel Brown Fellowship/Scholar-
  ship, 68
Radioactivity, xiv, 42, 44
Radioimmunoassay, 128, 136
Radioisotopes, xiv, 133
Research Corporation, 67, 68
Roentgen, Wilhelm, 44
Roosevelt, Franklin D., 89
Roosevelt, Mrs. Franklin D., 49
Roswit, Dr. Bernard, 133
Rutherford, Ernest, 44, 85

Sabin, Florence Rena, 7
  childhood and schooling, 31
  faculty of Johns Hopkins Univer-
    sity, 34
  honors and awards, 39
  mass tuberculosis survey in Denver,
    Colorado, 38
  medical school, 31
  received at the White House, 37
  research on tuberculosis, 37
  staff of Rockefeller Institute, 35
  statue of her given to Congress, 39
  work on lymphatic system, 33
  work on origin and development of
    blood vessels, 34
Sloan-Kettering Institute, 79
Speyer School, 60
Steward, Dr. Susan McKinney, 10
*Streptomyces noursei*, 67
Swallow, Ellen, 9
Swedish Academy of Science, 50
Szilard, Leo, 89
Szmant, Aline, 146

Taussig, Helen Brooke, 10
Taylor, Lucy Hobbs, 9
Tektite II project, 144–148
Teller, Edward, 89, 93
Thalidomide, dangers of, 10
Thorndike, Edward L., 56
Transmutation of chemical elements,
  46

*Index*

Transuranium elements, 46
Trotula, 3
True, Dr. Renate S., 145

Urey, Harold, 89, 93, 95

Vitamin B12, 108
Vitamin E, 77
Von Laue, Max, 110

Watson, J. D., xv
Walker, Dr. Mary Edwards, 7
Weisskopf, Victor, 89
Whitney, Eli, 5
Wigner, Eugene, 89, 96
Wilkins, Maurice, xv
Winters, Lawrence, 103
Wright, Corinne, 125
Wright, Jane C., 8
  associate dean of New York Medical
    College, 121
  cancer chemotherapy research, 119,
    120, 124
  children, 125
  early childhood, 118
  family background, 117
  honors and awards, 124–125
  marriage, 119

medical safari to Kenya, 120–121
medical school and internship, 118
President's Commission on Heart
    Disease, Cancer and Stroke, 121
residency in internal medicine, 119
Wright, Dr. Louis T., 99, 117

X-ray diffraction, 110

Yalow, Rosalyn S., xiv, xvii
  discovery and uses of radio-
    immunoassay, 136
  and Dr. Bernard Roswit, 133
  and Dr. Edith Quimby, 132–133
  and Dr. Solomon A. Berson, 133,
    138–139
  doctorate degree, 132
  early education, 129
  family background, 128
  marriage in 1943, 132
  Nobel Prize awarded 1977, 139
  received Albert Lasker Basic
    Medical Award, 139
  remarks on discrimination against
    women, 139–140
  teaching assistantship in physics,
    130

Zacharias, Jerrold, 129

Index

171